Henry Hartley

Hunter Explorer Extraordinaire
1815 - 1876

Ian H Mackay

TSL Publications

First published in Great Britain in 2022
By TSL Publications, Rickmansworth

Copyright © 2022 Ian H Mackay

ISBN / 978-1-915660-06-0

The right of Ian H Mackay to be identified as the author of this work has been asserted by the author in accordance with the UK Copyright, Designs and Patents Act 1988.

All rights reserved. No part of this publication may be reproduced, stored in a retrieval system or transmitted, in any form or by any means without the prior written permission of the publisher, nor be otherwise circulated in any form of binding or cover other than that in which it is published and without a similar condition being imposed on the subsequent buyer.

Cover images

Front: **"What led to the discovery of the Gold Fields"** this oil painting was painted in 1874 by Thomas Baines shortly before his death, in recognition of Henry Hartley's "accidental" discovery of an abandoned ancient indigenous gold quartz digging in 1865, while on an elephant hunting expedition to the Ndebele/Zulu Kingdom of Chief Mzilikazi in Matabeleland (in present day Zimbabwe)

Thanks to Michael Tucker, from the Zimbabwe History Society and author of the www.ZimfieldGuide.com website for contributing the image on the front cover (courtesy of the National Archives of Zimbabwe)

Back: the **"Giraffe Wearied"** painting of Henry Hartley by Thomas Baines, presented to HH by TB on September 14, 1869, sent to me by Anne-Marie Moore (nee Hartley) of her grandfather's grandfather.

Dedication

My last five self-published books were dedicated to my son, Michael Cordach Mackay, or to his son, Brendan James Mackay, born in 2013. Since then my dear wife, Diane, and I have been blessed with the birth of three delightful and equally enquiring granddaughters, Emily Kaur Mackay & Lilly Iris Weatherhead in 2016; and Clara June Weatherhead in 2018.

This book is dedicated to our grandchildren. They have all taken a keen interest in listening to their "Oupa" (grandfather) recite yet another enthralling story of Henry Hartley's mid-1800s elephant hunting escapades and pioneering explorations of southern Africa. They cross-examine him in detail as to each story's authenticity. I am teaching them to be very discerning of anybody trying to feed them "fake news" or misinformation of history.

Contents

Glossary of Afrikaans/Indigenous Words and Place Name Changes	7
Time line of notable events in Henry Hartley's lifetime	10
Acknowledgments	13
Prelude	15
Chapter 1: Introduction	19
Chapter 2: Family background - The 1820 English immigrant/settler	23
Chapter 3: The virile young gentleman	29
Chapter 4: Immigrating today is so different to the early 1800s	31
Chapter 5: Growing up in Bathurst, eastern Cape Colony	32
Chapter 6: Involvement in the Frontier Wars against the Xhosas	35
Chapter 7: The ox-wagon transporter between Grahamstown & Potchefstroom; and beyond	40
Chapter 8: Hunting advisor to Voortrekker Boers & close acquaintance of the future President of the Transvaal Republic?	44
Chapter 9: First tobacco growing farmer in South Africa at his *Thorndale* farm	49
Chapter 10: Entertaining host to wildlife hunters passing through *Thorndale* on their way north	50
Chapter 11: Medicine man & amateur surgeon in the bush	54
Chapter 12: An oft-told tale of Henry Hartley discovering the Victoria Falls BEFORE David Livingstone	56
Chapter 13: The fearless elephant hunter	60
Chapter 14: Trampled by a charging white rhinoceros	63
Chapter 15: Character & physical description as a mature adult	70

Chapter 16: Advisor and confidant to Ndebele/Zulu
King Mzilikazi and his successor Chief Lobengula 77

Chapter 17: Discoverer of ancient gold diggings in
central, present-day Zimbabwe in 1865 78

Chapter 18: Travelling companion and guide to British
Explorer Thomas Baines 84

Chapter 19: . . . And what became of his four hunting sons
and stepson? 108

Chapter 20: Current Hartley generation still farming
in the Magaliesberg 117

Chapter 21: Founder of the town of Hartley & Hartley Hills
in central Zimbabwe (Rhodesia) 119

Chapter 22: Concluding Commentary 120

Chapter 23: Postscript 122

Appendices 133
- Extract from 1846 Hartley Family Bible showing important dates
- Letter from David Livingstone to Thomas Baines, September 1858
- Anxious letter from Henry Hartley sent to Thomas Baines from Hartley Hills on July 4th, 1869
- Extract of Rhino sketch and rivers from Thomas Baines's original Field notes July 15, 1869, MS 049/9.2 , from page 90
- Agreement of mining concession, August 1871
- Copy of personal letter penned by Henry Hartley on August 20, 1870 on learning of the death of his third-born son, Willie, while elephant hunting near Hartley Hills - Courtesy of Ann-Marie Moore (neé Hartley)
- Exchange of correspondence relating to Mining company formation i.e. Letter dated 23, October 1874 from Thomas Baines to Henry Hartley
- Map of South East African Gold Fields by Thomas Baines of his exploits up to 1875
- Map of 1884 boundaries of colonial claims. "Africa South of the Equator" published in 1890
- Stanford's New Map of the Orange Free State and the southern part of the South African Republic, 1899, published by Edward Stanford, London, just before outbreak of the Second and deciding Anglo-Boer War – "The Crisis in South Africa"

Select Bibliography 147

Index 150

Glossary of Afrikaans/Indigenous Words & Place Name Changes

Bechuanaland – a British Protectorate that gained its independence as Botswana in the 1960s

biltong – a delicacy and staple diet of the Voortrekkers. Strips of venison or beef were dried in the open air shade and preserved with coarse salt, coriander and other spices, like North American jerky

beskuit – a hard baked biscuit that was often dunked in coffee, carried by horsemen to be eaten on the road as an early morning snack or minimal breakfast

Bittereindes – Afrikaner Boer guerilla warfare fighters who refused to give up after the formal end of hostilities of the Second Anglo-Boer War from 1899–1902

Botswana – formerly known as Bechuanaland

British Kaffraria – colony to the east of the Great Fish River annexed by Great Britain after the Frontier Wars between 1858 and 1894. The territory subsequently became part of the semi-independent Transkei Bantustan and then part of the Eastern Cape Province in post-Apartheid South Africa

Bulawayo – "Place of Slaughter", Royal Kraal of amaNdebele Chief Lobengula, present day capital of Matabeleland District in Zimbabwe

Chigutu – present day name of Hartley Town and Hartley Hills

Difaqane or Mfecane – period of tribal internecine conflict in pre-colonial times – including King Shaka Zulu expelling his challenging Lieutenant Mzilikazi northwards into the Transvaal from his Kingdom in Zululand in the early 1800s

Disselboom – the central pulling beam in front of an ox-wagon to which the oxen were attached

Fingoes – subservient sub-tribe of the Xhosa nation. After fleeing the genocide of Putinonic King Shaka Zulu in the early 1800s, the Fingoes later became allies with the British Colonialists against the predominant Tembu faction of the Xhozas

Gamyana River – often referred to in Thomas Baine's diaries. "The present-day Manyame river that flows east – west to the north of Hartley Hills (before turning north-west towards the Zambesi river) which the Baines/Hartley party left on 29 August 1869. Hartley Hills itself is on the Umfuli (present-day Mupfure) river". (*Source*: Michael Tucker at the Zimbabwe Historic Society)

Gqeberha – known as the city of Port Elizabeth prior to 2021

Grahamstown – garrison village and drosty established by the British on the eastern frontier of the Cape Colony in the early 1800s, now renamed "Makhanda"

Harare – capital city of Zimbabwe, formerly known as Salisbury in Rhodesia

Hartley town and Hartley Hills – named after its founder Henry Hartley by Explorer Thomas Baines, now known as Chigutu

Kariega – formerly known as Uitenhage

King William's Town – established by the British cColonialists in the 1800s outside the port city of East London in the Eastern Cape Province, recently renamed Quonce

Kruger, Paul – Voortrekker leader and President of the ZAR Transvaal Republiek until 1902, born in Cradock eastern Cape Colony on October 10, 1825

Makhanda – previously known as the Cathedral city and university town of Grahamstown

Mashonaland – vassal territory of Chief Mzilikazi and his successor Chief Lobengula. Inhabited by subservient Mashona tribesmen in the 1800s. Became allies with Cecil John Rhodes against the dominant Matabele in 1893 following constant cattle raids and plunder by Chief Lobengula and his warriors

Oudebaas – an affectionate nickname give to Henry Hartley – "the old man" by all who knew him

padkos – literally "food for the road" or a picnic lunch

Port Elizabeth – city established for English settlement in 1820 by the British colonialists in the Cape Colony on the Great Fish River frontier, and the main port of the Eastern Cape Province since then, now known as Gqeberha

Quonce – known as King William's Town prior to 2022

Rhodesia – named after Cecil John Rhodes, the Kimberley diamond magnate and Imperial sponsor of the British South Africa Chartered Company under a British Royal Charter, after defeating Chief Lobengula in 1893. Rhodesia was renamed Zimbabwe at the end of the civil bush war of the 1970s, when the country was granted formal recognized independence in 1980

riempie – leather strips, often made into a leather rope or for lining seats on furniture

Salisbury – capital city of Rhodesia, now known as Harare

Transvaal – Province within the Union of South Africa, after 1910 until 1994

trek – transportation by ox-wagon

Uitenhage – industrial town outside Port Elizabeth, now renamed Kariega

Uitlander – outsider from a foreign country

Umvolumo river – outside Hartley Town (*Source*: Michael Tucker at the Zimbabwe History Society)

vetkoek – literally a "fat cake". The Voortrekkers deep fried bread flour in boiling animal lard that was cooled and then carried for later consumption as high calorie padkos while trekking by ox-wagon or by horse

Voortrekker – Afrikaner pioneer

amaXhoza tribe – comprising Tembu, Pondo and Fingo factions in the 1800s

ZAR (Transvaal) Republiek – the independent Zuid-Afrikaanse Voortrekker Boer Republic, comprising the amalgamation of the Origstad, Zoutpansberg and Potchefstroom mini Boer states, formed after the Sand River Convention of 1852. When the British failed to annex the territory for Great Britain in 1879, the Imperialists lost the First Anglo-Boer War of Independence. The Pretoria Convention of 1881 recognized its self-governing independence once again, with only foreign affairs reserved to Great Britain. The ZAR remained an independent country, ruled by the Afrikaner Boers, until the end of the decisive Second Anglo-Boer War of 1899–1902. The country became the Transvaal Colony after formal surrender at the Vereeniging Peace Treaty signed on May 31, 1902, until it joined as the Province of the Transvaal within the Union of South Africa in 1910

Zimbabwe – formerly known as Rhodesia, and before that as the self-governing Southern Rhodesia Colony. It became part of the Central African Federation in 1953, together with the Northern Rhodesia Protectorate (Zambia) and the Nyasaland Protectorate (Malawi).

Time line of notable events in Henry Hartley's lifetime

1771 - Birth of Thomas Hartley (Senior) in Yorkshire, England, patriarch of the Hartley 1820 English Settler immigrant family, and father of Henry Hartley

1815 - Henry Hartley born in Mansfield, Nottinghamshire, England

1820 - Hartley family settled in Bathurst on the eastern frontier of the Cape of Good Hope Colony. Henry attended the Bathurst School and became fluent in Xhosa and Afrikaans

1833 - Married for the first time to Emma Witcomb Kidson

1837 - Henry became involved in the Frontier War of that year

1841 - Trekked to the Transvaal as an ox-wagon trader/transporter and started hunting wildlife professionally

1846 - Arrested in Origstad in the north-eastern Transvaal for "illegally" trading and hunting elephant as an uitlander

1846 - Established a permanent homestead on a pleasant, well-watered farm that he named *Thorndale*. in the protected Magaliesberg valley

1855 - Dr David Livingstone "discovers" Victoria Falls on the Zambezi river on his exploration walk across the subcontinent from the Atlantic Ocean to the Indian Ocean, to terminate the slave trade

1856 - Self-inflicted national suicide by the amaXhoza people in the eastern Cape frontier by starvation, after slaughtering all their cattle and burning all their crops following the counsel of a witchdoctor

1857 - Married for the second time, to Elizabeth Hope Upton

1860 - Married for the third time, to widow Mary Ann Maloney, with two Maloney children, which Henry Hartley adopted

1861 - Trekked to Lake Ngami and the Kalahari desert in Bechuanaland to hunt for ivory

±1864 Befriended King/Chief Mzilikazi of the amaNdebele/Zulu warrior tribe near Bulawayo and became his trusted advisor

1865 - Discovered probable ancient gold mining diggings while hunting elephants in Matabeleland. *(See illustration on front cover)*

1866 -	Explored gold diggings with German geologist Karl Mauch, to confirm the existence of payable gold, and travelled with him again the following year
1867 -	Rich diamondiferous geological pipes discovered at Kimberley
1868 -	Chief Mzilikazi dies at his Royal Kraal at Inyati near Bulawayo
1869 -	April 1869 to December 1870. First Expedition to Matabeleland with Explorer Thomas Baines. April 9, 1869. Thomas Baines, with the help of Henry Hartley obtains verbal agreement from the interim Matabele Regent to prospect for and to mine gold in Matabeleland and part of the adjoining vassal territory of Mashonaland
1869 -	November 26. Rhino tramples and seriously injures Henry Hartley. Treks back to *Thorndale* to recuperate for several months
1870 -	January. Lobengula proclaimed King/Chief of the amaNdebele tribe in Matabeleland
1870 -	May 1870. Henry Hartley's third, and favourite biological son, Willie, dies at the age of 17 of fever while hunting elephants in the lowveld areas below the higher elevation Hunter's Road to Hartley Hills, pioneered earlier by Henry Hartley. Henry only arrived at the hunting camp in Hartley Hills in August 1870 to learn of the tragedy for the first time
1871 -	May 1871 to March 1872. Thomas Baines' Second Expedition to Matabeleland. Henry Hartley only accompanies Thomas Baines to the Tati gold diggings in July 1871, where Henry turns around and treks back to his *Thorndale* farm in the Magaliesberg, and to explore for alluvial diamonds
1875 -	Thomas Baines dies of dysentery in Pietermaritzburg, Natal Colony, on April 8
1876 -	Henry Hartley dies on his *Thorndale* farm in the Magaliesberg on February 8
1887 -	Anglo-Zulu War and the Battle of Isandlawana in the Natal Colony in which "Harry" Hartley (Henry Hartley's youngest biological son) plays a prominent role
1899 -	October 12. Start of Second Anglo-Boer War. Thomas John Hartley, second biological son of Henry Hartley killed in a skirmish at Ladysmith, fighting on the Boer side against the British Imperialists
1902 -	May 31. Formal end of the Second Anglo-Boer War.

Acknowledgments

I was most fortunate to have the enthusiastic, remote assistance of **Desré Stead** and **Jennifer Kimble** at the *Brenthurst Library* in Parktown, Johannesburg. With her methodical and diligent investigative talents, Desré uncovered **priceless original primary source documents** for me from the archival collection. These included actual correspondence of Henry Hartley, and original notebooks, correspondence, maps and diaries of Thomas Baines. Jennifer was instrumental in helping me proceed to publication.

Simon Hartley (born 1968), a direct paternal descendant, kindly provided me with hundreds of pages of Hartley Family genealogical history, photos of artifacts and anecdotes compiled by family members and passed down from one generation to the next. Simon's grandfather's grandfather is Henry Hartley. Simon still has the 1846 Hartley Family Bible signed by his famous ancestor, containing pertinent information. Simon and his family still live on a farm in the Magaliesberg, not too far from the ancestral *Thorndale* farm.

I was also fortunate to have incisive input from **Jane Carruthers**, Professor Emeritus of History at the *University of South Africa* in Pretoria. Jane is an expert on Thomas Baines and has written extensively on this well-known English Explorer of southern Africa, who visited and consulted with Chief Lobengula at his Royal Kraal in Matabeleland from 1869 to 1872. Her expertise further contributed to my knowledge of their interactions with Henry Hartley.

Cécile Verseput, another direct descendent, has a huge beautifully glazed porcelain teacup and accompanying saucers in her collection. (See photos in Chapter 10). Henry Hartley almost certainly used that crockery to entertain and knowledgeably advise his Voortrekker Boer big-game hunter friends at his *Thorndale* farm homestead – on their way north during the winter hunting seasons of the 1860s and 1870s.[1]

Anne-Marie Moore (neé Hartley) kindly shared original correspondence, paintings and important family documents. Anne is a direct descendant of Frederick Hartley, Henry's eldest son.

Thanks too to **Brian Wood** and **Diane Mackay** for perusing and improving the final drafts.

---

[1] By carefully examining the Registration Mark on the underside we were able to positively confirm that the cup and saucers emerged from Kiln #13 on November 25, 1868 of a Midland English porcelain manufacturer.

Prelude

During our seemingly never-ending Covid-19 to Covid-22 global pandemic, I discovered and became intrigued with an English elephant hunter by the name of Henry Hartley (1815–1876).

Hartley was blessed with a superb intellect, developing multiple divergent skills and talents. Besides his southern African exploration ambitions, he was a pioneering tobacco, citrus and coffee farmer, and showed bravery as a hunter of very wild rhinos, elephants, buffalo and lions.

He was notorious for his keen sense of self-deprecating humour, his embellished campfire yarns, hunting stories and wildlife encounters.

It is known that Henry Hartley could easily converse with, and was trusted by the Zulu-related, Ndebele tribes up north near the Zambezi River, because there are many similarities with the Xhosa (Nguni) languages that he absorbed growing up as a child in Bathurst in the Eastern Cape in the 1820s. He became a trusted advisor and confidant to the Nedebele/Zulu Chief Mzilikazi in Matabeleland, and his son Chief Lobengula who succeeded him in 1870.

Hartley was the first white man to visit many significant parts of southern Africa that even Dr David Livingstone missed the same missionary-inspired era, and the same wild geographic locale. Hartley was not a missionary, nor an elected leader, but nevertheless a noble, well-liked, helpful fellow who met and interacted with many of the important political players of his time – who have themselves been written about *ad infinitum*. Hartley became a prolific professional elephant hunter.

Yet, there is no published, comprehensive biography on this English 1820 Settler and southern African Explorer pioneer – just lots of bits and pieces of interesting information, and "sidebars" scattered everywhere in the historic record.

I have perused hundreds of original documents and secondary articles from the period. The *Brenthurst Library* in Parktown, Johannesburg, was of great assistance in downloading digital copies of the easy-to-read, handwritten, copious Victorian script of fellow explorer Thomas Baines (using a constantly-sharpened graphite pencil) and more rarely of Henry Hartley (using a quill ink pen). These documents provide exceptional *insight* into the friendly, cooperative manner of Henry Hartley and his ambitious entrepreneurial *foresight*. (In *hindsight* Henry Hartley should not have shot all those gentle, majestic elephants for their ivory!! – but it was a different, "non-environmental", historic era in the 1800s).

While hunting with Hartley, fellow traveller/explorer Thomas Leask writes[1] that "Hartley says he intends 'collecting all his manuscripts and getting them published'". That never happened, because the British Imperial soldiers burned down his *Thorndale* farm homestead and its contents during the Anglo-Boer war in 1899. (See later).

The more I discovered of Henry Hartley the more I realized what an incredibly kind and helpful individual this visionary gentleman was in his time, and within the context of that turbulent historic period – across all races, warring tribal/colonial leaders, ethnic groups, languages, divergent cultures and political perspectives. We can all learn valuable life lessons from his character and moral traits. It did not matter whether they were black or white, English Imperialist or Afrikaner Boer, Ndebele or Shona, Xhosa or Zulu. He was not a politician.

Henry Hartley was 150 years ahead of his time in racial and ethnic conciliation. That is the theme of this book, which I wish to explore, communicate and expand on.

If we do not learn from history to live together peacefully and co-operatively, as Hartley demonstrated during his life time, we will continually repeat the mistakes of accumulated history.

The character and human interactions of this "unknown" 1820 English Settler and Southern African Explorer Extraordinaire deserves his own biography.

Henry died at the relatively young age of 60 from prior injuries sustained in an encounter with a white rhinoceros charging him after being shot. Today, the eradication of the tsetse fly, black-water fever, and deadly malaria have allowed humans to safely access these previously almost uninhabited, low-veld, wild, big-game regions. Protection of wildlife was not a pressing issue in the 1800s. It definitely is now!

I obtained a facsimile reproduction of the 1877 edition of *The Gold Regions of South Eastern Africa*, written by Thomas Baines F.R.G.S., three volumes of *The Northern Goldfields Diaries of Thomas Baines 1869-1872*, edited by J.P.R. Wallis in 1946, and a detailed print copy of a large, monochrome (100cm by 75cm) 1876 Map of Southern Africa that Baines compiled. I also purchased many books and journals

---

[1] Leask, Thomas, *Southern African Diaries* of 1865–1870, edited by Wallis, 1954. Entry for Sunday, July 15, 1866 on p. 73

written by other contemporary explorers who travelled with Hartley during that era, including Eduard Mohr and Thomas Leask.

The original dairies/fieldnotes of Thomas Baines kept at the *Brenthurst Library* were used in the compilation of that 1876 Map, and are the basis of his iconic historic 1877 book.

As a result I was able to dispel many of the on-going falsehoods, myths and misinformation written about this iconic elephant hunter and explorer, and also gained fresh insights into this era of southern African history. It was a wonderful Covid project to keep me busy in "self-isolation".

Chapter 1:

Introduction

Who was Henry Hartley?

Unfortunately, all memory of his achievements have been eradicated by modern politicians. Place names have been altered, plaques and statues in his memory have been vandalized and destroyed. It is as if he did not exist.

Yet, Henry Hartley had a profound impact on the development of southern Africa. Not a political office-bearer, but a natural diplomat. He nurtured friendly relationships with everyone he met, *whether they were black or white, Anglo or Boer, Xhosa or Zulu, Matabele or Shona.*

An English immigrant to the Cape of Good Hope, and the first European to explore central Zimbabwe[1] in the 1860s, and reveal its natural wealth?

I began researching the life of this incredibly well-connected and influential, but sparsely-written-about gentleman – born in Nottinghamshire in 1815, who came to Port Elizabeth/Algoa Bay[2] with his parents as a 1820 English settler.

Here are some highlights of his life . . .

- British-born, Henry was the second youngest of eleven siblings;
- As a young 1820 English immigrant he grew up and was schooled in Bathurst, Cape Colony;
- a multi-linguist, he became fluent in English and Afrikaans, and several Nguni bantu languages, including Xhosa, Zulu and Ndebele;
- he was involved in skirmishes with the Xhoza "Kaffirs" in several Frontier Wars;[3]
- apprenticed as a blacksmith with his father and elder brothers;

---

[1] Then known as Matabeleland and Mashonaland.
[2] Which changed to a new name "Gqeberha" in 2021, with difficult-to-pronounce Xhosa clicking sounds for most inhabitants of South Africa who use English as their primary language.
[3] In South Africa, "Kaffir" is now an antiquated derogatory racial term for describing supposedly uneducated, Xhoza warriors/defenders along the Eastern Cape Frontier.

- became an ox-wagon trader between Grahamstown[1] and Potchefstroom in the interior selling finished goods in exchange for valuable ivory and wild animal skins;
- Hartley became the most prolific elephant hunter ever, supposedly killing over 1,200 elephants personally[2] in the north-western Transvaal, Bechuanaland, and the future Rhodesia;
- became an acquaintance, if not a personal hunting friend, of future Transvaal Republic President Paul Kruger, and was – unusual for an English "Uitlander"[3] – granted almost immediate ZAR Transvaal Republiek citizenship. Paul Kruger may have been instrumental in granting him the large, prime, middle-veld farm, between Rustenburg and Pretoria, that he named *Thorndale* when he first arrived as an ox-wagon trader between Grahamstown, Potchefstroom and Rustenburg in about 1841;
- was a self-taught "pharmacist", medical "doctor", and a proficient amateur surgeon in the veld – using traditional Victorian, Voortrekker and African bush remedies;
- had difficulty walking with a club foot, but was an excellent marksman and horse rider;
- always helped other people in dire situations, no matter what their background was;
- was a personal advisor and trusted confidant to the exiled warrior Ndebele King/Zulu Chief Mzilikazi in Matabeleland near Bulawayo[4] around 1860 to 1865 – (and his successor Chief Lobengula in 1870). Mzilikazi was the challenging nephew of the infamous Shaka Zulu warrior king and had to flee northwards with his faction and followers to escape execution and annihilation;
- was instrumental in the "rediscovery" of abandoned ancient tribal gold diggings in Matabeleland, and adjoining Mashonaland in 1865 – and later passed on those secret locations to the forerunners of Cecil John Rhodes and his Rhodesian Pioneer Column of his Imperialist *British South African Concession Company* – granted by Queen Victoria;
- took the reputable geologist and German Explorer, Dr Karl Mauch with him in 1866 to Matabeleland (the future Rhodesia) to confirm gold quartz findings;

[1] Now renamed "Makhanda".
[2] Not substantiated. Could be as "low" as a few hundred elephants!
[3] An "outsider" from a foreign country.
[4] Meaning "Place of Slaughter".

- took the famous 1800s painter/illustrator/prospector Thomas Baines with him on his exploration/hunting trips to Bulawayo and Hartley Hills in Matabeleland (and the future Rhodesia) from 1869 to 1872 to record significant cultural happenings and zoological/botanical observations, and prospect for gold;
- was severely injured by a charging – normally placid – white rhinoceros in 1869;
- semi-retired after that major accident to his well-known *Thorndale* tobacco, citrus and fruit farm that he established in the Magaliesberg mountains, 47 miles west of Pretoria;
- he died there at the age of 60 in 1876, and is buried on his *Thorndale* farm;
- his third son Willie died of black-water fever in Matabeleland at the age of 17 years while hunting elephants with his father in 1870;
- his eldest son, Frederick, was involved in fighting the Afrikaner Boers on the British side;
- his second son Thomas John was killed in a skirmish during the *Siege of Ladysmith* fighting on the Boer side in the second Anglo-Boer War in 1899;
- his youngest son "Harry" (Henry Albert Rorke) was involved in fighting the Zulu impis in Natal at Isandlwana in 1879, and the Anglo-Boer War of 1899-1902, on both sides of the conflict.

There is an extensive listing of published and unpublished sources on Henry Hartley at the end of this book.

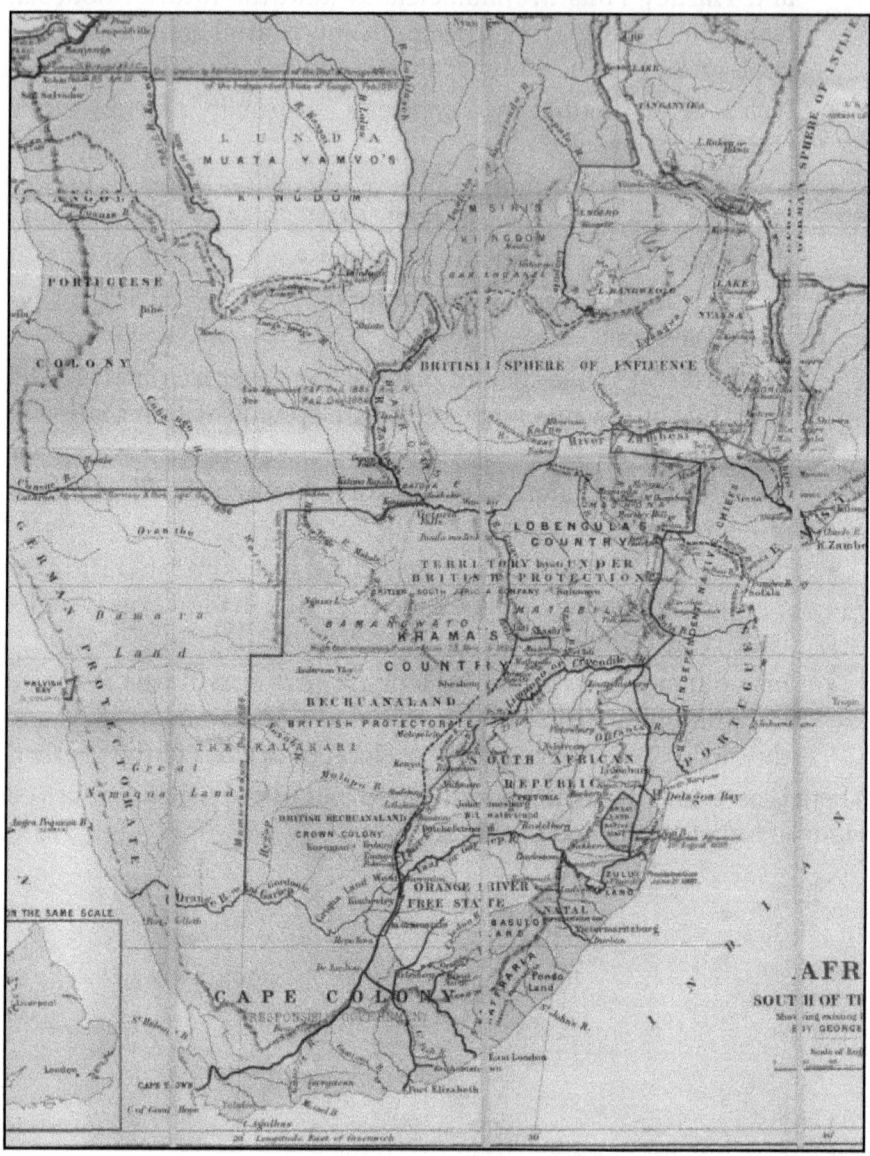

Extract of map of southern Africa showing boundary treaties after the Berlin Conference of 1884 that divided Africa into European colonies and Spheres of Influence (From Rare Maps)

Chapter 2:

Family background:
The 1820 English immigrant/settler

Henry Hartley, "The Hunter", was born in 1815 in Mansfield, Nottinghamshire, England, south of Sheffield.

Along with most of his nine older siblings and one younger sister he was baptized in the Anglican Parish Church of St Peter & St Paul in Mansfield. The original church dates back to the 1300s and communion is still celebrated with the congregation. His father, Thomas Hartley (Senior) was born on January 10, 1772 in the same market town.

Henry's two older brothers, William and Thomas (Junior) worked at their father's forge. They were all blacksmiths. His father Thomas (Senior) married a widow, Sarah Green – Henry's mother – after his first wife, Hannah, died in England. His sisters, Mary, Ann, Hannah, Elizabeth and Sarah probably worked in nearby knitting mills as loom operators.

Economic conditions were tough in the English Midlands after the end of the Napoleonic Wars with so many soldiers returning home and growing young families to feed. Rapid mechanized industrialization eliminated much manual labour previously required during the feudal era for the same output.[1]

Great Britain had taken over control of the Cape of Good Hope from the Dutch in 1799, creating emigration opportunities for a potentially better life.

Thomas Hartley (Senior) and Sarah Green choose to enlist in the Emigration Scheme.

The Hartley family set sail for South Africa in early 1820.

Besides working with his father as a blacksmith in the Mansfield forge, Thomas (Junior) – a much older brother of Henry's – was a dedicated 17-year-old student of medicine for Dr Calton on their difficult 107-day-long sailing voyage to Simonstown and Algoa Bay

---

[1] This introductory section is mostly based on a two-hundred-and-twenty-four page Hartley family history manuscript provided to me by Simon Hartley (b. 1968) on his famous grandfather's grandfather. It was diligently compiled by Aileen Berrington and later printed by M&M Printers in Queenstown, Eastern Cape Province, as *The Hartley Story: Thomas Hartley Senior and his sons Thomas Hartley Junior & Henry Hartley ("the hunter")* in 1987.

on the small sailing vessel, *The Albury*, crammed with immigrant families. Thomas (Junior) assisted Dr Calton in the medical treatment of fellow passengers and developed a special aptitude by borrowing books on medicine from the doctor's on-board collection. Brother Thomas spent hours reading up on the subject while at sea. Dr Calton was the sponsor and leader of the immigrant group, but sadly died shortly after arriving in the Colony.

Unlike today, with social media on the Internet providing instantaneous news to prospective refugees and other migrants of conditions on the ground in the new country, the passengers on the *Albury* had virtually no idea of what to expect when they landed in their new country. Little did they know that the Immigration Plan was to "place a body of sturdy men on the turbulent eastern Frontier of the Cape Colony with the object of forming a 'human shield' against marauding Black Tribes who dwelt beyond the Great Fish River of the Colony".[1]

There were no black bantu tribes permanently settled in the winter rainfall or arid Karoo areas of the western Cape of Good Hope. Only a scattering of Khoisan nomadic Bushmen and Hottentots greeted the Dutch East India Company Commander Jan van Riebeeck when he landed at Table Bay on April 6, 1652 to establish a "refreshment station" and build a secure fort to protect the newcomers. These Stone-Age aboriginal peoples, who arrived in the Cape more than 25,000 years ago, mostly died out from small pox and other deadly diseases that the European settlers brought with them – or were integrated through interbreeding. Slavery was common until the British put a stop to that practice in the early 1800s. The Dutch imported slaves from Malaysia to work in their homes and on their farms in the Cape.

The Cape Khoisan nomadic hunter/gatherers were colloquially known as "Bushmen" with bows and arrows, or beach-scavenging "Strandlopers". The Hessequa were nomadic pastoralists wandering the countryside in animal skins with an ox to carry their flimsy worldly goods, and a few sheep. They were known as "Hottentots".

The Xhoza and Zulu Nguni-speaking Bantu living in the summer-rainfall eastern and northern parts of South Africa were pastoralists and agriculturalists, growing sorghum, maize and vegetables planted in the warm summer rainfall areas. These Iron-Age black warrior tribes migrated down from central and west Africa perhaps 8,000 years ago. They also kept large herds of cattle for meat and milk, and as a source of wealth. This cattle wealth was also useful in acquiring

---

[1] Berrington, Aileen, 1987, p. 7

the best wives by paying *lobola*.[1] They were also assegai-throwing and spearing warriors who often raided each other to steal or recover stolen cattle, take over the defeated warriors' wives and enslave their children. The Great Fish River traversing the eastern Cape from north to south was a natural boundary line between the summer-rainfall and winter-rainfall regions of South Africa, but was easily crossed.

As European settlement expanded eastwards, frontier villages such as Grahamstown and nearby newly-settled farms came under increasing attack from warring, amaXhosa coming across the Fish River to raid their farms, burn down their homesteads and steal their cattle and sheep. Inevitably this led to counter raids by settler commandos on horseback to retrieve their livestock and perhaps steal the Xhosa livestock as a reprisal. A never-ending cycle of attack and counterattack.

Thus a Scheme for Emigration and Colonisation was formulated to send 4,000 English settlers to the eastern Cape from Britain in 1820. The thrill of going to a new, sun-blessed country with the promise of 100 acres of land attracted nearly 9,000 applicants, including Thomas Hartley Senior and his brood.

The terms of the Scheme were as follows:[2]

1. Only groups of ten or more able-bodied men (persons) under the leadership of a responsible person would be accepted.
2. They were to be sponsored by someone with the necessary means to pay.
3. The sponsor would have to pay Deposit money of £10 Sterling for every family of 1 man, 1 woman and 2 children; £5 for every 2 children under 14; and £5 for every single person 14-18 years taken out.
4. A passage would be provided at the expense of the government, who
5. Would victual the settlers for the duration of the voyage.
6. Each able-bodied settler was to be allocated 100 acres of land on a quit-rent basis payable after the first three years of occupation.
7. To look after the spiritual welfare of the settlers, the government would pay the stipend for a minister of religion for each party exceeding 100 able-bodied persons.
8. The deposit money would be refunded to the settlers on the following conditions: one third after landing, one third when settled on the land, and one third three months from date of location. Payment to be made in the necessities of life, not in cash. (This latter clause was

---

[1] A dowry to the bride's father.
[2] Berrington, Aileen, 1987, p. 7

imperfectly understood by some of the colonists, causing trouble soon after landing, as many expected cash payments).

Thomas Hartley Senior and his brood were chosen to sail with Dr Calton's Party of Settlers, embarking on the *Albury* sailing vessel from Liverpool on January 28, 1820. They were amongst the 4,000 approved immigrants. Thomas applied to take two and a half tons of iron ingots on board to forge into useful trade goods once he arrived in his new country. The *Albury* arrived at Simon's Bay just south of Cape Town on May 1, 1820 to take on drinking water, fresh supplies and yet more immigrants transferred from the settler ship *Zoroaster* for the remaining leg of the voyage to Fort Frederick on Algoa Bay. The party finally disembarked there on May 15, 1820 after 107 days, or nearly four months, at sea. (Nobody was permitted to disembark at Simonstown for fear of spreading onboard contagious diseases to the local population).

The Dr Calton Party was then transported by ox-wagon to the Torrens River for final settlement on their 100-acre surveyed allotments on July 26, 1820, north-east of Bathhurst. The settlers were indentured to their sponsors for several years and had to pay quit-rent. The Hartley family were allocated two farms, both filled with thick thorn scrub and little surface water to occupy and defend against Xhosa cattle rustlers from across the Great Fish River. There was no easy way of turning back to their home country across the oceans again. Dr Calton unexpectedly died shortly after arriving at their final destination.

Henry Hartley was a six-year-old child at the time.

The second eldest brother, Thomas (Junior), who was twelve years older than Henry, was a stable, guiding light to young Henry, especially in the early period in Bathurst following immigration to the wild Eastern Cape. Thomas (Junior) cheated his age by one year to also qualify as an adult for 100 acres of land in their new country. Their father Thomas (Senior) was approaching the relatively "old age" of 50 by the time they were fully settled in Bathurst.

Thomas (Junior) was an accomplished emergency medical practitioner in their new settlement from his medical knowledge gleaned from Dr Calton while at sea for such an extended voyage. Slowly, through hard work and ambition he continued as a blacksmith, farmer, healer, extractor of teeth, churchgoer, public-spirited committee member, auctioneer, shopkeeper, pharmacist and pound master. The family established a large retail and wholesale general store in Bathurst, opened in 1834. (Aileen Berrington itemizes an extensive inventory and wide range of diverse Victorian-era goods available for sale in the shop).[1]

They also owned two inns, several farms and became very active in the ox-wagon trade of export goods to the hinterland and the import of ivory, ostrich feathers and animal skins from the wild north. (This was before the arrival of railway lines from Port Elizabeth and East London to the hinterland in about 1892, which subsequently completely disrupted the highly profitable ox-wagon transport trade business and made that pedestrian mode of long-distance transport obsolete).

Thomas (Junior) built and owned the "Pig & Whistle" pub in Bathurst. The pub sadly had to close down during the Covid-19 pandemic in 2020, after operating successfully there as a business for nearly two-hundred years. There are currently no buyers for the business. The historic village itself is suffering from poor municipal governance and lack of infrastructure maintenance.

Grahamstown was the administrative frontier town in the eastern Cape Colony. Like most towns in South Africa it was designed with very wide streets – wide enough to allow a full span of oxen to turn around with its wagon. The village soon had a Drosty,[2] Garrison, gaol, and a cathedral. Several secondary education, religious-based boarding schools were built to accommodate farmers' children.

Bathurst, established in 1820, was a mere hamlet, a day's travel by ox-wagon on rough roads to either Port Alfred or Grahamstown.

The initial settlers built rudimentary "wattle and daub" homes for themselves from wattle lattice strips and wet clay, reinforced with cattle dung and straw as a binding medium in the absence of concrete. They topped the home with joists, cross beams and thatch grass. The internal and exterior walls were neatly plastered with wet clay and dung and regularly washed with limestone to give them a white appearance. The floors were laid down with clay and dung and polished by hand to an attractive, smooth shiny finish, in the manner of local Xhosa rondavels. Stone, concrete, and kiln-fired clay-brick buildings followed in later decades with corrugated-iron roofs.

The settlers were familiar with this type of construction, used in England during the Tudor era. Concrete came later.

Without a doubt Henry was brought up in a very ambitious, financially-astute, close-knit family environment. After finishing elementary school, he probably accompanied the local commandos in the numerous Frontier skirmishes against the Xhosa tribes across the Great Fish River. Henry learnt to ride a horse at an early age, became

[1] Berrington, Aileen, 1987, pp. 26-32
[2] Magistrates Court.

an expert marksman and hunter of wildlife, especially elephants, ostriches, lions and rhinoceros. He was already a successful transport trader between Grahamstown and Potchefstroom, and renowned elephant hunter by the age of 24.

Henry married for the first time to Emma Whitcombe Kidson when he was 18 and she was 15.[1] Her older sister Mary Anna had married Thomas Hartley (Junior) some five years earlier. Thus, brothers married sisters.

---

[1] Berrington, Aileen, 1987, p. 187

Chapter 3:

The virile young gentleman

Besides being an accomplished horseman, tracker, marksman and hunter, Henry Hartley was also a virile, energetic, astute young gentleman. He supposedly had a head of blond hair and piercing blue eyes.

He married young, and then often.

Henry married three times.

His *first marriage* at 18 years of age to fellow teenager Emma Kidson was celebrated in the newly-completed Wesleyan Church in the hamlet of Bathurst in 1833. Their first reported child was Sarah Ann born six years after their marriage, which was unusual for that time. Children were often conceived soon after marriage. A sister, Mary Elizabeth, arrived two years later.

Frederick was born in 1844.[1] He accompanied his father and brothers on hunting expeditions, and became a prominent tobacco, citrus and fruit farmer in the Magaliesberg valley.

Thomas John was born in 1846. Thomas inherited the family farm *Thorndale* following the death of William in 1870 and his father in 1876.[2] He was an odd character. He had married an Irish-influenced Maloney, who encouraged him to join the Boers against his British heritage and was killed in action in 1899. He had the misfortune of listening to this anti-English brother-in-law, who was also his stepbrother, and fought on the side of Afrikaner Boers against the British.

Thomas John Hartley lost both his farm and his life as a result of this "disloyalty" to Queen Victoria in that conflict.

William (Willie) was born in 1853. This favourite son died while on an elephant hunting trip at the age of seventeen from black-water fever in the hot Lowveld elevations below the "Old Hunter's Road" before his father arrived by ox-wagon on the same hunting expedition with explorer Thomas Baines.[3] He is buried at Hartley Hills, which later became part of the country of Southern Rhodesia. Seven

---

[1] Died in 1902.
[2] It is not known why Frederick, as the eldest surviving son, did not inherit the family farm.
[3] William succumbed to this deadly fever while on a hunting expedition on May 29, 1870, Baines, Thomas, Journal of 1877, p. x

other hunters in the party died within days of each other of tropical diseases on the same trip.

Henry Hartley's *second marriage*, by special licence in 1857, was to Elizabeth Hope Upton. She died on the *Thorndale* family farm in the new Transvaal Republic only two years later during childbirth.[1]

Henry's *third marriage*, at the Presbyterian Church in Grahamstown in 1860, was to Mary Ann Maloney (née Rorke) a widow. She already had two Maloney children, which Henry adopted. This included Tom Maloney – about the same ages as his biological sons, Frederick, Tom and William – and accompanied them and his step-father on his many hunting trips to Matabeleland. This third marriage produced an additional son, "Harry", **Henry Albert Rorke Hartley**, and a daughter who died as a child.[2]

---

[1] Berrington, Aileen, 1987, p. 23

[2] The original Henry Hartley family bible from 1846 was given to his fourth son, Henry Albert Rorke Hartley. Born at *Thorndale* farm on November 21, 1861 Henry Rorke is Simon Hartley's great, great grandfather. The 1846 family bible is still in the possession of the current Hartley family and records some important dates and events.

Chapter 4:

Immigrating today is so different to the early 1800s

In today's interconnected world of instantaneous Internet communication to anywhere in our global village it is much easier to migrate, legally or illegally. Social media often paints an allure of booming economies and generous government handouts for would-be migrants. They are often in mobile telephone communication with family and friends already settled in the country they intend to move to. You can even walk-in or arrive as a zodiac boat refugee to a western country with a well-developed welfare system within the European Union, Britain and North America.[1] Facilitated by profiteering people smugglers, millions of destitute individuals from Africa, the Middle East and Central America have in recent decades relocated to escape civil unrest, criminality and despotic ruling regimes in the countries of their birth.

Today, potential economic migrants still have to prequalify with rigorous entry requirements as formal immigrants before gaining admittance, just as the 1820 English settlers did, but do not need to take a hazardous four-month sailing trip across the Atlantic and Indian oceans to get there.

Today, potential international migrants set off across the Mediterranean from North Africa to Europe, or across the narrow Channel from France to England on flimsy inflatable boats to be picked up by a western country, and potentially granted asylum and resettlement in a host country. They pay the illegal people smugglers anything from 1,000 to 5,000 Euros per passenger for the one-way dangerous sailing, generally without lifejackets. The inflatable floating boats or decrepit obsolete fishing vessels are often used only once before being confiscated by the border authorities on arrival.

---

[1] 28,000 Haitians were arrested trying to cross the US-Mexico border between October 2020 to August 2021 – *Wall Street Journal*, September 22, 2021.

Chapter 5:

Growing up in Bathurst, eastern Cape Colony

Henry had to overcome a "severe physical handicap in that he was club-footed in both feet".[1] Other references say that he was only partly handicapped in one foot. But, he was an energetic, strongly-built young child, determined to overcome his physical disability.

Growing up in the Bathurst (Albany) district of the Cape Colony frontier Henry Hartley and his teenage school friends quickly became skilled at riding horses and handling rifles alongside the menfolk, in defending their family homesteads and farms from constant threat of attack by the Xhosas raiding across the Great Fish River.

The Wesleyan Church in Bathurst, which the Hartley family attended, opened for public worship on May 8, 1832, and was used as a refuge during the Frontier Wars.

Henry would have played with some of the domestic Khoisan- and Xhosa-speaking children in the employ of his parents and elder siblings in the backyard and become highly proficient in mastering the strange dental, lateral, and alveolar, clicking sounds of the Xhosa language, which is common to Nguni-group languages such as Xhosa, Hottentot, Zulu and Ndebele. His fluency in these languages, as well as English and Afrikaans, proved invaluable when negotiating and trading with the Afrikaner Boers in the Transvaal and with King Mzilikazi and Chief Lobengula in Bulawayo Matabeleland, in his adult years.

Like most 1820 Settler children he also attended elementary school to learn the three R's of Reading, Writing and Arithmetic at the local Bathurst School. The village Wesleyan school was run by the Rev. Boardman. Henry was blessed with an astute, attentive brain, a superb grasp of events, diplomacy, and friendly persuasiveness. He developed a beautiful cursive handwriting style. Examples of his writing can be found in an anxious letter dated July 4, 1869, written to Thomas Baines on a hunting/expedition trip to Matabeleland, and a sad letter dated August 20, 1870 addressed to his eldest son, Frederick, announcing the unexpected death of his young brother, Willie, while on an elephant hunting trip. (See Appendices).

[1] Le Roux, *Servaas. Pioneers and Sportsmen of South Africa*, 1939, p. 91

The Blacksmith

The young Henry Hartley apprenticed as a blacksmith just like his elder brothers, and father Thomas Hartley (Senior) before him. It was a much sought-after and essential skill in a new frontier country. We know that Thomas Hartley (Senior) asked permission to bring 1.5 tons of iron ore ingots with him on the *Albury* immigrant sailing ship in 1820. As part of the immigration agreement he had to pay *quitrent*, or goods in kind, for the 100 acre farm he was allocated to occupy in order to obtain full freehold title. Thomas (Senior) was most annoyed that his working tools were held back in trust in a warehouse and that he had to "buy them back" to release him from this obligation.

The male family members would have been skilled in forging horse harnesses, picks, spades, riding stirrups, horse shoes, wagon axles and be as proficient as a wheelwright in manually beating an ox-wagon outer wheel rim into the appropriate circumference and shape for fitting to a wagon wheel or Cape Cart. A wide range of iron tools and metal farm implements would have had to be manufactured from scratch in the new country. They would have had to also manufacture two-bore and four-bore lead and tin slugs for elephant guns.

Henry Hartley did not forget his blacksmith trade as a professional elephant hunter, nor his desire to help his friends in need. Thomas Leask in his diary entry for August 23, 1870 writes: "Mr Hartley welded my waggon tyre (wheel rim) and I made a new disselboom, so that the waggon is set up again".

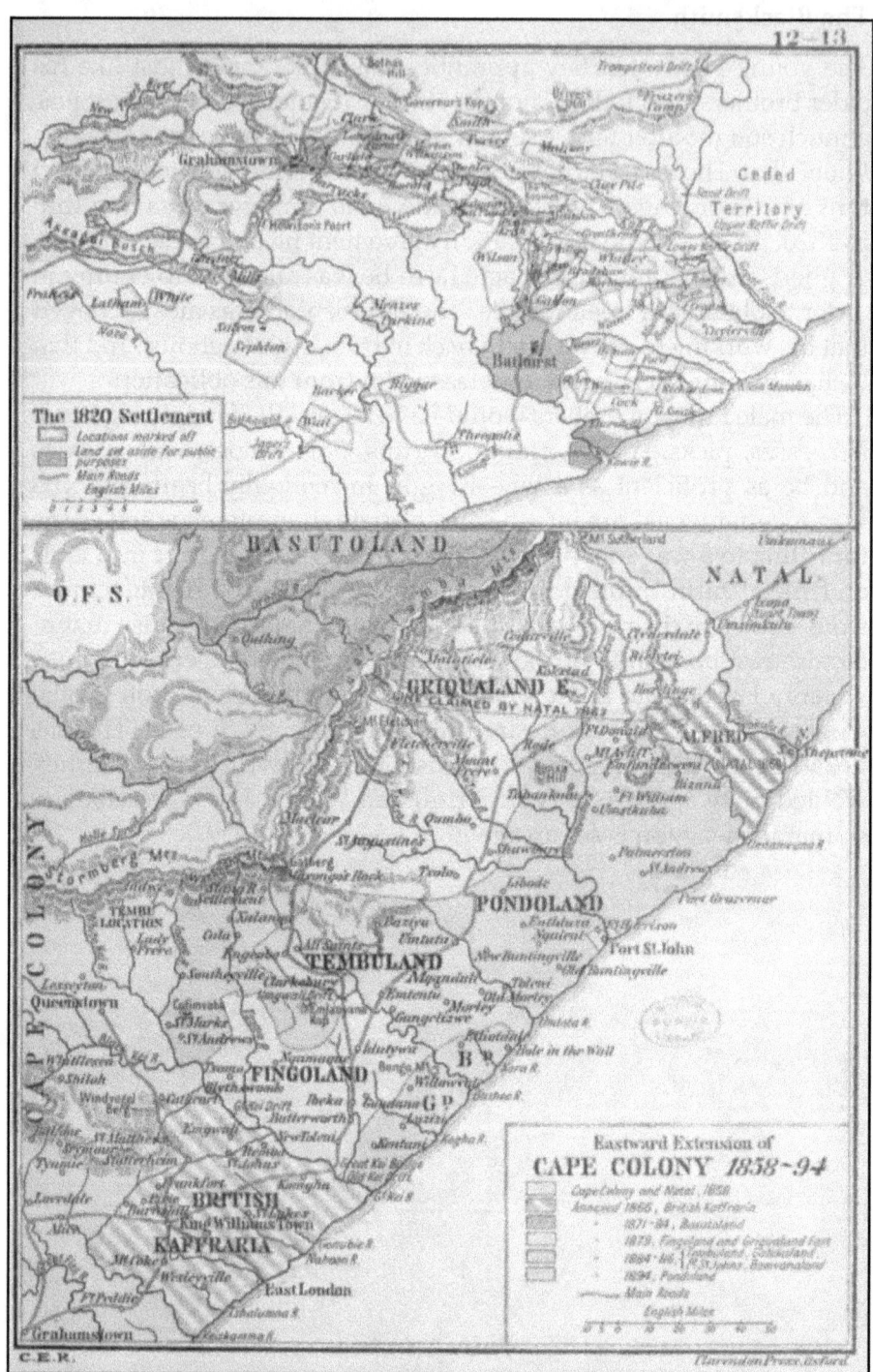

Map showing 1820 Settlement and Eastward Extension of Cape Colony in 1858–1894: 12-13
(*Historic Atlas of South Africa* by Eric A. Walker, 1922)

Chapter 6:

Involvement in the Frontier Wars against the Xhosas

In his diary entry for September 22, 1834, Jeremiah Goldswain (a fellow 1820 Settler) and Sunday School Superintendent at the Wesleyan Church in Bathurst, reports that he had English, Xhosa and "Hottentot" children in attendance at his Sunday School classes. There was no blatant racism amongst the new English Settlers. Henry's elder brother by twelve years, Thomas Hartley (Junior) was a regular congregant and later appointed as Steward and Treasurer of the Chapel.[1]

Then everything changed with an attack from the east.

The new settlers were enjoying the long warm days of summer with crops and fruit orchards ripening. Their herds of cattle and flocks of sheep had produced new calves and lambs. Jeremiah was as busy as ever hauling loads of lime on his ox-wagon from his kiln to customers as part of his transport business. Plum puddings were baking in the Settlers' wood-fired, kitchen ovens. But, by Christmas Day, war had broken out yet again between the Settlers and the assegai-throwing Xhosa warriors, some now with breech-loading hunting rifles.

The tribesmen were intent on avenging the recent killing of their Xhosa Chieftain Maqoma's brother by Cape Mounted Rifles. The warriors raided on foot in their thousands, killing many Dutch and English colonial farmers, burning down or destroying their homesteads and driving away stolen cattle and sheep eastwards across the Great Fish River. Again, in accord with their culture, the Xhosa warriors killed the men, but often spared the lives of white women and children. Homes in the little village of Bathurst were burnt down or ransacked, and families had to flee to Grahamstown, 24 miles to the north. These included the family farm homestead of Thomas Hartley (Senior) – the father of Henry Hartley – and the homestead of Jeremiah Goldswain.[2]

A counter attack was launched. Volunteer Dutch and British colonist commandos, British troops from the Grahamstown Garrison, and Khoi forces on horseback with rifles rode eastwards to retrieve their

[1] Berrington, Aileen, 1987, pp. 22, 25 & 88
[2] Goldswain, Jeremiah, 1858, edited by Ralph Goldswain, 2014, pp. 90 & 101

stolen livestock. The Xhosa tribesmen were defeated, and livestock retrieved. The area between the Great Fish River and the Great Kei River was annexed to become "British Kaffraria" with King Williamstown as its capital. Hostilities subsided.

I cannot find any confirmation of Henry Hartley actually fighting combats in any of the several Xhosa Frontier Wars.

He was 19 years of age during the important Sixth Frontier War of 1834 so would have been eligible for conscription. Henry was certainly exposed to the sporadic and regular skirmishes with the Xhosa tribes from across the Great Fish River, that served as the nominal boundary between the British-ruled white Cape Colony and black-ruled Xhosas. As a conscript he would have had to fight alongside the local Bathurst commandos in retrieving stolen cattle and sheep from raiding Xhosa warriors, and defend the family homestead against attack.

The British troops were later helped in their annexation of the territory beyond the Great Kei River by the Fingo faction. The Fingoes had assimilated with and become subservient to the dominant Tembu faction of Xhosa tribesmen, after being defeated by and fleeing Shaka's Zulu armies in the early 1800s.[1]

The *Nongqawuse* or national suicide of 1856 and 1857 from across the Great Kei River in Transkei

9/11 is a significant historic date in Manhattan New York City, when on September 11th, 2001 Islamic zealot, suicide pilots almost simultaneously flew four passenger jets into the World Trade Centre and the Pentagon. It is amazing how a single significant event can change the course of history in a country.

Who of you knew that after eighty plus years of intermittent raids and counterraids between the eastern Cape Colonists and Xhosa tribesman across the Great Fish River – known as the Frontier Wars – the Xhosa people committed national suicide in 1856 and 1857? It changed the course of history in South Africa. A paramount Xhosa Chief, Sarhili, under the superstitious spell of a young female teenage witchdoctor, by the name of Nongqawuse, prophesized that by killing all their cattle and destroying all their crops, the ancestors would come back from the afterlife and provide an abundance of food, livestock and prosperity on February 18, 1857. On that day the sun would rise in the west and set in the east and the Xhosas would drive all the white people into the sea.[2] Of course, nothing happened on

---

[1] Goldswain, Jeremiah, 1858, edited by Ralph Goldswain, 2014, p. 113
[2] Berrington, Aileen, 1987, p. 35

February 18th. The cult belief continued for a while, enforced by Sarhili.

In his personal account of *The Nongqawuse*, 1820 Settler Jeremiah Goldswain[1] writes in his memoirs of 1858 that starvation and disease resulted in tens of thousands of Xhosa people perishing when the prophecy did not materialize. He reports finding starving tribesmen dying along the sides of the roads, eating roots and grasses, and begging for food. The survivors flooded into the Colony and became indentured servants and tenant farmers on white settler farms. (Jeremiah Goldswain and his family, coincidently arrived as 1820 Settlers in the same ship on the same day at Algoa Bay together with young Henry Hartley and his family.)

A faction of subordinate Fingo Xhosas who resided mostly in adjoining British Kaffraria (and were often allies to the British and at war with the predominant Tembu faction of Xhosas) were better prepared for famine.

The Ninth "Kaffir" War from 1877 to 1879 consolidated British control over the eastern Cape Xhosa territories right into Zululand beyond Durban.

Fingoland in 1876 is a wonderful example of great advances made by the Fingo people when private property ownership was granted to individual black farmers by the Cape Colony.

Granting freehold land title to black farmers in British Kaffraria across the Great Fish River, and beyond the Great Kei River in Fingoland and what became known as the Transkei, enabled those Xhosa peoples to generate agricultural income directly for themselves. Some enterprising black farmers became wealthy, opened private bank accounts and were able to purchase teams of pack oxen, wagons, ploughs and other farm implements to become more productive. They were able to build more substantial dwellings for their families. By 1879 the magistrate of Umzimkulu noted that there were 8,000 individual native Xhosa farmers working 90,000 acres of land in his administrative district.[2]

Although the black farmers were pleased, this change did not go down well with the traditional Xhosa chieftains. The rigid tribal system of common ownership began to crumble. The absolute authority and power of the chief was diminished and his cattle wealth reduced. Their influence amongst their people diminished.

---

[1] Goldswain, Jeremiah, 1858, edited by Ralph Goldswain, 2014, p. 31
[2] Acemoglu, Daren & Robinson James A., *Why Nations Fail – the Origins of Power, Prosperity and Poverty*, 2012, pp. 258-271

Also, the white settler farmers in the Cape Colony did not like these new independent farmers competing on an equal basis to sell their produce on open markets. The whites found it increasingly difficult to obtain cheap labour to work on their farms from across the Great Fish River.

The right of individual registered land title was taken away by the Native Land Act of 1913 when the whites had stopped fighting each other in the Anglo-Boer War and had formed the Union of South Africa together. Under the Land Act, 87% of the land in the Union was reserved for white occupation, who comprised 20% of the population. 13% of the land was reserved for black Africans under traditional communal tribal ownership. A dual economy reemerged that enabled whites in the burgeoning mining and agricultural sectors to prosper, while facilitating the importation of poor black African unskilled labour from the traditional, communally-owned native tribal reserves.

This was the beginning of institutionalized Apartheid, resulting in a rigidly controlled, racially-based dual economy that lasted until Nelson Mandela became President with majority rule in 1994. The dual economy enabled whites to become affluent while impoverishing blacks, Indians and Coloureds.

Land Apportionment in Rhodesia in 1970, between land for white ownership, land for black ownership, and Tribal Trust Land under communal chieftain ownership was similar.

By the year 2000, Robert Mugabe – President of Zimbabwe (formerly Rhodesia), a Mashona – made the economic situation even worse. He began confiscating productive white-owned farms, and throwing the remaining 3,000 white commercial farmers off their land without compensation and allocating the land to his veteran political buddies. After being a bread basket for the supply of grains to southern Africa, the economy collapsed, and inflation spiraled out of control. The currency became worthless and the common people destitute. Democracy was soon replaced by a corrupt, self-serving régime under Robert Mugabe. The country and its economy have not recovered.

By the year 2000, Thabo Mbeki – President of South Africa of Xhosa descent – refused to reinvest in the State-owned Electricity Supply Commission and other parastatals. This led to their functional collapse, and ongoing electricity blackouts to this day. He and the African National Congress majority government adopted a racial policy of reverse Apartheid with its so-called Broad-Based, Black Business Economic Empowerment (BBBEE). Racism was reintroduced and previously-entitled white people were discriminated against in the award of government contracts. Meritocracy was not a consideration. Political connections were paramount. When Jacob Zuma – a traditional Zulu polygamist – replaced Mbeki as President in 2008 he took BBBEE to its next regressionary level. He focused on self-serving corruption called "State Capture" of almost all state contracts for himself, his family and a group of personal friends – especially the three Gupta brothers. They escaped the country the minute Cyril Ramaphosa took control to avoid prosecution. Zuma was incarcerated in jail for refusing to face long-standing corruption charges. His attempted insurrection in KwaZulu-Natal and Gauteng provinces in July 2021 was a failure.

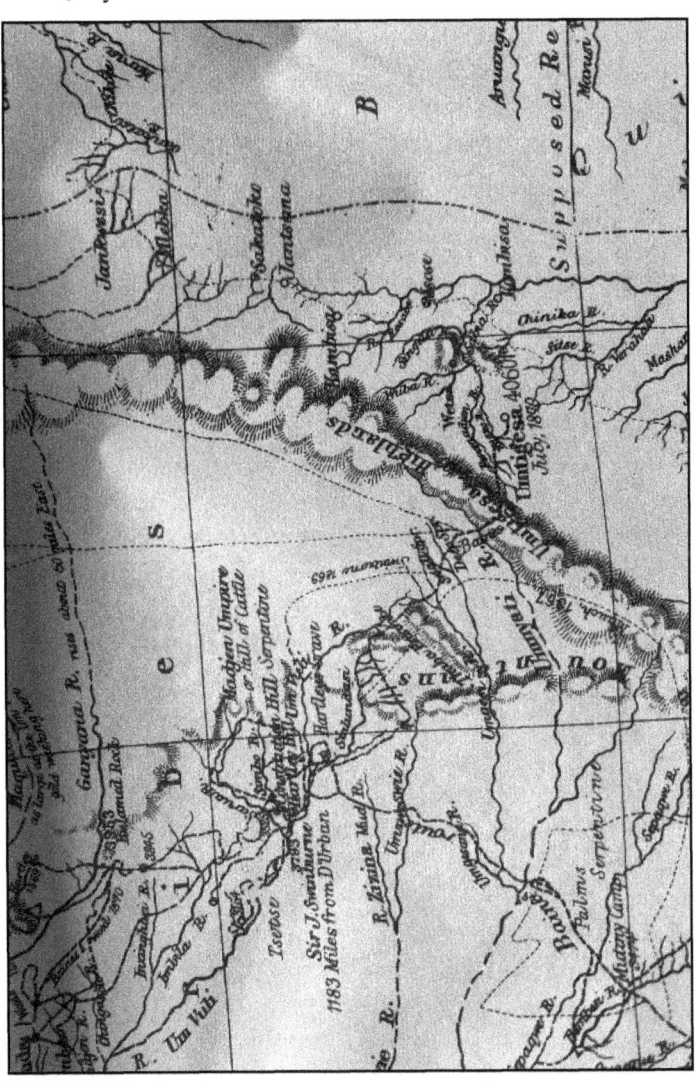

Extract of 1876 map showing location of Hartley Hills outpost and *Thorndale* farm in the Magaliesberg.

Chapter 7:

Ox-wagon transporter between Grahamstown & Potchefstroom; and beyond

There was busy trade by ox-wagon from the sea port of Port Elizabeth – the well-stocked Hartley family general store in nearby Bathurst with its wide range of Victorian goods – including the export of ivory, ostrich feathers and wild animal skins from the north, through the newly-established Transvaal Republiek capital at Potchefstroom, back to Grahamstown.[1] Henry became an ox-wagon transport rider around the age of 19, and a professional hunter at the age of 26 when he moved permanently to the north-western Transvaal in about 1841.

Most of the ivory that had not yet been hunted to virtual extinction by white European settlers in the western and eastern Cape Colony was purchased by barter from overtly hostile native tribes to the north occupying Zululand, Matabeleland, Mashonaland and Barotseland. It was the practice of native tribes to corral and herd their wild prey into narrowing, disguised passages, and then drive them over a hidden ledge into a steep, deeply-dug pit large enough to hold several elephants. They could then be slaughtered for their ivory and skins with assegais and spears for barter and export to European ox-wagon traders, like Henry Hartley.

Trekking by ox-wagon with a heavy load was a frustratingly slow means of transport. A wagon was typically pulled by six in-spanned oxen that could travel only as fast as a man walking – or about a maximum of 20 miles per day. The drag animals needed to graze, rest and drink at each outspan to regain their energy for continuing the journey. This further delayed progress.

If you were an observer looking down from outer space you would observe a slow-moving "train of caterpillars or centipedes" stretched along a 2,000 mile, rough gravel trading route into southern Africa,

---

[1] Grahamstown was recently renamed "Makhanda" – after the Xhoza advisor to Xhosa Chieftain Ndlambe in his failed attack on the British Garrison at Grahamstown in 1819. The tiny garrison village of Grahamstown with perhaps 30 houses was attacked by over 10,000 Xhoza warriors and defended by 330 armed men, of when 80 were Hottentots. The raid failed dismally. At least 700 Xhoza impis died against 3 dead and 5 wounded on the British side. (Bond, John, *They Were South Africans*, 1956, p. 33)

all the way from Grahamstown – Potchefstroom – Rustenburg – Tati – Bulawayo – Inyati – and terminating at Hartley Hills, near present day Harare (Salisbury) in central Zimbabwe (Rhodesia). If you focused in you would see a bright string of campfires at each outspan burning all night to keep the lions at bay from the oxen and horses. The travelers would be cooking dinner, warming themselves from the cold, and telling yarns or writing journals and letters.

The wagons would be loaded with finished Victoria-era goods and dry provisions going north and almost overloaded with valuable ivory and wild animal skins coming south. Postal items would be carried back-and-forth between the outspans by "Post Office" runners on horseback or by foot. It was almost like a spinal, slow-moving, interconnected city!

On the other hand, a man riding on horseback could travel about 50 miles each day. If you used a fresh horse each day you could travel up to 100 miles in a single day.

Captain Reginald "Henry" Hartley, whose maternal grandfather was Henry Hartley, tells us that his father Joseph William Thackeray (1837–1912) performed a return journey from *Thorndale* farm via Potchefstroom to his farm homestead in Cradock (520 miles) in 1863 in just "eight days – 65 miles per day – riding two horses alternately".[1] Sadly, Captain Thackeray is renowned for making up false myths, unsubstantiated conjecture, spreading misinformation and exaggeration of his boyhood idol and maternal grandfather.

Many will recall the heroic ride by a young Dick King[2] "famously completing a journey of 600 miles in 10 days on one horse" from the British-held port of Durban to the British Garrison in Grahamstown in the eastern Cape Colony. Both the newly-established, but land-locked, Voortrekker Boer Republics of the Orange Vriej Staat and the ZAR Transvaal Republiek needed access to a safe seaport. A Boer commando, led by Andries Pretorius, laid siege to Durban in 1840, in preparation for invasion. Dick King's bravery enabled the British to quickly send a military relief party by ship from Port Elizabeth to Durban and changed the history of South Africa forever, because the Boers could not establish their own external port. The British annexed Natal in 1843.

When the 3 foot 6 inch-wide Cape Gauge railway line was laid from Port Elizabeth and East London into the interior around 1890, steam locomotives pulling rail carriages completely disrupted ox-wagon transportation on the main trading routes. The ox-wagon became

---

[1] Thackeray, Reginald "Hartley" Thackeray, Henry Hartley: African Hunter and Explorer, appearing in the *Journal of the Royal African Society* of July 1938, p. 288

[2] Dick King was also an 1820 Settler and hunter/trader.

obsolete almost overnight. Telegraph wires were laid alongside the railway lines at the same time.[1]

In 1841, the ever-entrepreneurial Henry was one of the first ox-wagon transport riders to recognize that by avoiding the "middle man" and hunting for ivory directly himself he could substantially increase his net income, when he arrived back in Grahamstown to market his ivory.

But, the hostile native tribes had to either be defeated (as the Voortrekker Afrikaners only partially attained in the vast new Transvaal Republiek) or licenses to hunt within their sovereign tribal jurisdictions had to be negotiated beforehand with their paramount chief (or king) and his indunas. This is where Henry Hartley's astute mind, patience, kindness and diplomatic genius paid off enormously.

Not so for the Matabele nation thirty years later when British Imperialist Cecil John Rhodes and his Rhodesian Pioneer Column invaded the sovereign territory and mowed down the warrior tribesmen in their thousands in the 1890s with newly-invented Maxim machine guns. The Matabele warriors carried long assegais, knobkerries and broad spears. They were unaccustomed to handling breech-loading rifles. Emboldened with the muti (traditional Zulu tree medicine) given to them by witchdoctors they erroneously believed that the deadly bullets would rain down harmlessly.

Hartley, was the first white man to gain the trust of the exiled Ndebele/Zulu King Mzilikazi at his royal kraal at Inyati (near present-day Bulawayo) in the early 1860s. A number of other Afrikaner, English and German-speaking adventurers were then able to follow his diplomatic example and *modus operandi* with the warrior Matabele King to obtain hunting licenses within his territory. So close was the trust between Hartley and the Matabele paramount chiefs that a mere introduction by Henry Hartley was often adequate.

This also led to ox-wagon trips to Matabeleland by Karl Mauch, Eduard Mohr, Thomas Leask, Sir John Swinburne and Thomas Baines in the company of Henry Hartley for exploration and gold prospecting purposes in the late 1860s and early 1870s. Thomas Baines and Henry Hartley, in particular, became very good lifelong friends.

Thomas kept a detailed personal diary and made field notes on every smidgeon of new information that he came across; an impres-

[1] On July 9, 1873 the Cape Colony government made an agreement with Hooper's Telegraph Company in London to extend the submarine communications cable from Aden to Mauritius to Durban, to Port Elizabeth and to Cape Town. Soon telegram message exchanges between Europe and southern Africa became instantaneous – Mohr, Eduard, 1876, p. 437

sive legacy for us today. He created a huge detailed map of his explorations and prospecting trips to southern Africa, and wrote a Journal summarizing his exploits to 1875 – both published posthumously in London in 1876 and 1877. His 1860 to 1875 Southern African diaries were edited and published by J.P.R. Wallis in 1941 and 1946. All of Henry Hartley's personal records of his explorations and hunting/prospecting trips were destroyed during the Anglo-Boer War in 1899, so we know very little directly from Henry Hartley.

The purpose of Baines's trip was to again meet with Chief Lobengula and confirm the verbal agreement that he had reached for a gold mining permit the previous year on April 9th for all of Mashonaland – but this time in the form of a formal, legally-recognized and assented to, written agreement that he could take back to London with more samples for assaying their worth.

Chapter 8:

Hunting advisor to Voortrekker Boers, & close acquaintance of the future President of the Transvaal Republic?

Henry Hartley and Stephanus Johannes Paulus (Paul) Kruger were in a similar age demographic, had similar hunting interests and lived in the same Rustenburg, Magaliesberg area from 1841.

Paul Kruger was born in Cradock in the Cape Colony on October 10, 1825.[1] He was a revered leader of the Afrikaner *volk* ("people" in Afrikaans, German and Dutch), becoming State President of the Republic (in 1883) after the successful defeat of the British Imperialist forces at Majuba Hill, who were trying to unsuccessfully annex the Transvaal for Queen Victoria. After the London Convention of 1884 with Great Britain, the Transvaal regained its independence, but was subject to the suzerainty of Great Britain for its foreign affairs.

Paul Kruger trekked up to the Transvaal with his family and the Voortrekker Potgieter Party in 1836 and was granted his first farm *Waterkloof No.4* along the banks of the Hexriver near Rustenburg in 1842 at the age of 16! It was the practice of the newly-established, self-declared Republic to grant "two farms to new farmers in the initial years of white settlement in the Transvaal (ZAR)".[2]

Henry Hartley was a newly-arrived British English 1820 Settler and ox-wagon trader between Grahamstown – Potchefstroom – Rustenburg and Magaliesberg and Pretoria around 1841, and a professional elephant hunter. Granting him a trading licence in the Afrikaner Republic proved to be controversial, but as a professional elephant hunter he must have been regarded as an asset to the Voortrekkers.[3]

Notwithstanding that he was an English "Uitlander" (an English foreigner from the British-ruled Cape of Good Hope Colony) and that there were laws forbidding any Englishman or German from owning land in the new Republiek he was soon granted burgher citizenship and was also granted two farms. He chose *Thorndale* farm on the

---

[1] His birthday was celebrated as a statutory public holiday from 1882 to the start of the Second Anglo-Boer War in 1889 and again from 1952 until 1994, when Nelson Mandela became President of South Africa.

[2] Bergh, 2014, p. 69

[3] Bulpin, T.V., 3rd Edition, 1974, p. 67

strong, perennial Magaliesspruit, on the southern fold of the Magaliesberg/Witwatersrand mountain range, west of Krugersdorp. It was located on the old ox-wagon trading route between what would become Pretoria, and Rustenburg through the narrow Olifant's Nek Pass – a very good location for his ox-wagon transporter business through Potchefstroom to Grahamstown, and his elephant hunting expeditions to the north.

He also acquired a farm in the Groot Marico area of the north-west Transvaal, which he used as an operational base for his hunting trips further north.[1]

It is very probable that Henry Hartley and Paul Kruger were hunting acquaintances, if not good friends.

As the officially appointed young *Veldt Kornet* for the Rustenburg District, Kruger preferred to be paid in farm grants of land rather than in Treasury-issued bank notes, because of their unstable and depreciating exchange value. He did not even keep a banking account at that time. He was later appointed as Commandant and Commandant-General and became interested in politics. He also led several burgher commando raids against rebellious bantu tribes, who survived the Zulu warriors.

When the Voortrekkers arrived to settle as farmers in the Orange Free State and Transvaal the highveld grass plains had been mostly "swept clean" during the *Mfecane* ("the crushing") and *difaqane* ("the scattering") period of Zulu King Shaka. These grassland areas were almost devoid of human habitation as a result of the genocide carried out by King Shaka Zulu and his Zulu lieutenant Chief Mzilikazi as he fled north to the area around Bulawayo in advance of the Potgieter Voortrekkers – allied with pockets of defeated Tswanas, Basothos, Vendas, Bechuanas, Malalaka, Pedi, Shangaans and Moshonas. The main body of Zulu warriors under "Napoleonic" Shaka Zulu and his successor Dingaan retreated to their traditional homeland in northern Natal.

Chief Mzilikazi was the founder and king of the conquering Matabele nation. Eight years younger than Shaka Zulu he rose to the position of general in Shaka Zulu's army with eight full regiments of 100 men each under his command.[2] He was brave and ruthless. Opposing tribesmen were surrounded and massacred to the last standing man. Even the mixed-race Griqua nomadic pastoralists who identified themselves with the Cape colonists were annihilated.[3] The *raison d'être* of his regiment was to conquer or die. You faced execu-

---

[1] Le Roux, 1939, p. 88
[2] Ritter E.A., *Shaka Zulu*, 1955, pp. 168 & 201
[3] Rittter, E.A., 1955, p. 325

tion for retreating in the face of the enemy. Maidens of defeated tribesmen were carried off as booty. Each warrior or impi was awarded with up to 500 cattle. He rewarded a few of the best stolen cattle to lower warriors, and the most number to higher level indunas in the hierarchy, with the right to breed with the King's prize bulls. Within a generation or two of selective cross-breeding the genetic quality of the entire herd would be enhanced.

But, Chief Mzilikazi got over-ambitious by challenging the Zulu king. King Shaka drove him out of Zululand at the beginning of the 1800s to maraud across the plains of the future Orange Free State, Transvaal and Bechuanaland, committing genocide.

When the white Afrikaner Voortrekkers trekked northwards around 1835 they were able to ally themselves to the defeated bantu remnants. Boer commandos then drove the Mzilikazi Zulu faction northwards across the Limpopo River out of the Orange Free State and Transvaal, where Mzilikazi established the northern Ndebele/Zulu kingdom of Matabeleland.

At that time black people were treated as compliant manual labourers by the white European settlers, or at best as second-class citizens with no right to vote, unless they were well educated in the European way, or owned property.

Copy of watercolour by Thomas Baines
of Afrikaner Voortrekker practice of "Inboekseling"

One of the reasons for the Afrikaners leaving the Cape Colony in the 1830s was to get away from British rule and the newly-pro claimed Abolition of Slavery Act throughout the Empire and the world. The Afrikaners did not themselves officially own slaves, but surviving women and children of defeated tribes sometimes became indentured domestic servants and farm workers or tenants on their new farms in the Transvaal and the Orange Free State.[1]

Some of the aggressive Voortrekker Afrikaners treated black tribesmen as subservient, sub-humans, who could even be killed at will or indentured as farm labourers with little or no consequence of retribution from the government.

Should Henry Hartley and Thomas Baines have intervened in the Afrikaner Boer *Inboekseling* caravan practice if they were present and observed it? Raiding resident black tribes, stealing their cattle, pushing them off their land and indenturing their surviving women and children was a despicable barbaric practise even during the *mfecane* and *difaqane* killing and dispersal period.

This depiction of Afrikaner "*Inboekseling*" in 1870 in the ZAR Transvaal Republic that Thomas Baines painted to "prove" that Afrikaners were cruel to the defeated surviving black women and children is most likely propaganda! Baines was known for disseminating British disinformation. False myths and misinformation were just as prejudicial in 1870 as they are today. I learned from reading page 487 in his diary, September 16th, 1870, that he never actually witnessed what he painted in that horrific scene of "undisguised slave trading", and admitted that "most Dutchmen would treat them with less cruelty; (than the local black warrior chiefs after battle). and . . . I made a sketch of the waggon from Mr. Wood's description". i.e. based on third-hand anecdotal information, NOT on first-hand observation! Never instantly believe what you read in the newspapers or see on TV, whether it comes from 1870 or 2022.

However, proof that this practice did occasionally occur as an isolated incident comes from none other than missionary/explorer David Livingstone himself. Sechele, a Bekwena chieftain in the western Transvaal was attacked by Transvaal Boers in 1852. "They killed many of the Bakwena and carried two hundred children into

---

[1] There were indentured servants and tenant black farmers on white commercial farms until the end of Apartheid in the late 1980s. Cecil John Rhodes did try to grant "Equal rights for every civilized man south of the Zambezi" as part of his grand, but self-serving Imperial vision for Africa. (See p. 613 of Cambridge History)

captivity".[1] They were taken to their farms as "apprentices", "tenant farmers" and "indentured" servants.

In the period to 1877 when the British Imperialists first annexed the young, disorganized and virtually bankrupt Afrikaner Boer Republic, Kruger acquired ownership of at least twenty-seven farms in the Rustenburg District alone.[2] Afrikaner Boer leaders in different parts of the Transvaal were also constantly at political loggerheads with each other. There was no cohesive or effective united governance. Government business concessions were rife with corruption.

But, Paul Kruger was a stubborn, stoic defender of his Afrikaner people and devotedly religious. He and his Voortrekker family belonged to a more austere faction of the Protestant Calvinist faith, known as "Doppers".[3] This ultraconservative offshoot followed a stricter interpretation of Calvinism that was introduced by the Dutch Rev. Dirk Postman to the Rustenburg congregation, attended by Paul Kruger. They renamed themselves the *Gereformeerde* (re-reformed) *Kerk van Zuid Afrika*, or *Nederduitsche Hervormde Kerk* (Dutch Reformed Church). They preferred reciting Psalms from their large Family Bibles from the Old Testament rather than readings from the New Testament. Singing hymns was considered improper. Sundays were sacrosanct, reserved for worship. No sport was played on Sundays. Dancing and drinking alcohol was frowned upon. They believed in pre-determination. They also strongly believed that they were the Chosen People of God to lead their volk into the Promised Land.[4] The *Hervormde Kerk* became the official State Church of the Transvaal Republic in 1859. They were staunchly anti-Catholic.[5]

The more traditional and less austere Calvinist *Nederduitshe Gereformeerde Kerk* (Dutch re-Reformed Church) in the Cape Colony, followed the same ecclesiastical principals as Scottish Presbyterianism.

---

[1] Leask, Thomas, *Southern African Diaries of 1865–1870*, edited by Wallis, 1954, p. 38, quoting Livingstone's *Missionary Travels*, p. 33
[2] Bergh, 2014, p. 70
[3] derived from the old Dutch word "Domper" – one who damps down. P. 138, Rosenthal, 1978.
[4] Bulpin, 1974, p. 90
[5] As a "hard-headed" individualist, Paul Kruger may have displayed many of the egoistical, belligerent and bombastic characteristics of isolationist, modern-day, Donald Trumpism.

Chapter 9:

First tobacco growing farmer in South Africa at *Thorndale* farm

With his innovative flair, Henry Hartley experimented with growing citrus, coffee and tobacco on his fertile *Thorndale* farm along the Magalies River Valley. It was one of the first farms to be granted to white settlers in the new Transvaal Voortrekker Republiek. The farm has its own microclimate, protected from the cold winter winds blowing from the south by a leeward slope of the Witwatersberg in the Magaliesberg mountain range. As a result, Henry's lower elevation, middle-veld lands were mostly frost free.

The farm possessed an adequate supply of fresh perennial water that emerged from an underground stream on the adjoining *Maloney's Eye* farm. That farm was owned by Tom Maloney (Senior) before he died young.[1] The underground stream had its origins at Sterkfontein Caves twenty kilometres to the south-west, just outside Krugersdorp,[2] and inherited by his widowed wife, Mary Ann Maloney (neé Rorke). Mary married Henry Hartley (also a widower) in 1860 when she became a widow with two Maloney children of her own, including Tom Maloney (Junior). Tom would regularly go hunting with Henry Hartley to Matabeleland with Hartley's three eldest biological sons in the late 1860s and early 1870s.

Henry was able to entertain his guests with pipe tobacco and manufactured cigarettes from the tobacco that he harvested and cured on the farm.

His eldest son Frederick carried on the commercial farming businesses, and also used the tobacco juice for dipping cattle.

Henry was granted a second farm around 1846, in the Groot Marico region in the western Transvaal on the Bechuanaland border. Situated on the Marico river it was used as a staging base for Hartley and his friends' elephant hunting trips to the north. Today the area comprises the privately-owned Madikwe Wildlife Preserve according to Ann-Marie Moore (neé Hartley) – a direct descendant.

---

[1] *Maloney's Eye* farm, also known as *Derdehoek*, was previously owned by Koos de La Rey, a Voortrekker and prominent Transvaal Afrikaner Boer War General.

[2] Meaning "Strong fountain" in Afrikaans. This is where the world-famous fossilised skull and skeleton of "Mrs Ples" was dug up almost intact by Wits University palaeontologist Robert Broom in 1947. "Mrs Ples" was an upright-walking homosapien antecedent.

Chapter 10:

Entertaining host to wildlife hunters passing through *Thorndale* on their way north

Although hunters went north to Lake Ngoma and Bechuanaland to hunt, the territory of Matabeleland, ruled by King Mzilikazi, was a "No Go" area for European settlers until Henry Hartley "broke the ice" and befriended the tribal king. The winter months from March to October were the best months climate-wise for Europeans.

Besides helping the Afrikaner Voortrekkers to hunt in areas to the north of the Transvaal, where ivory and valuable wildlife were not yet extinct by the 1850s; and leading the German geologist Karl Mauch and British explorer Thomas Baines on mineral prospecting expeditions in the late 1860s – where payable gold had not yet been confirmed – Hartley also became a personal advisor and trusted confidant to the exiled warrior Ndebele/Zulu Chief Mzilikazi and his successor Lobengula in Matabeleland at Bulawayo and Inyati.

Simon Hartley mentioned that his grandfather's grandfather almost certainly used colossal porcelain teacups and accompanying saucers to entertain and graciously advise his Voortrekker Boer big-game hunter friends at his *Thorndale* farm homestead – on their way north.

One of Simon's anecdotes handed from generation-to-generation – in the traditional "Zulu" way of historic story telling – is that Henry Hartley personally had them glazed and kiln-fired for him, transported by ship to Port Elizabeth and then by ox-wagon to the Magaliesberg; and then had some of the ceramic saucers "welded" to the ceramic teacups as he was irritated by a particular Boer "lack of etiquette". While giving valuable tips on hunting and how to negotiate with Ndebele (Zulu) Chief Mzilikazi at Bulawayo, he often served the Boer hunters with *koffie-en-beskuit* from 1846, who were trekking through his Magaliesberg farm. They would pour their hot coffee or tea into the saucer to cool it down and then drink/slurp it directly from the saucer in a very un-English, non-etiquette manner. Henry Hartley was not impressed.

Queen Victoria was also riled by President Paul Kruger when he poured his hot tea into the delicate china ceramic saucer at the Palace to cool it down before drinking-slurping the tea directly from the saucer when he tried to negotiate full independence for the Transvaal ZAR Republic with her at the Pretoria Convention in London in 1881. The Transvaal Republiek remained under British suzerainty for its foreign affairs. Perhaps with a proper understanding of British tea-drinking etiquette Paul Kruger may have negotiated a better deal for his people?

Another direct descendent, Cécile Verseput, still has some of those iconic tea cups and saucers in her collection that she had inherited from her maternal grandmother, and kindly provided me with some photographs. See below . . .

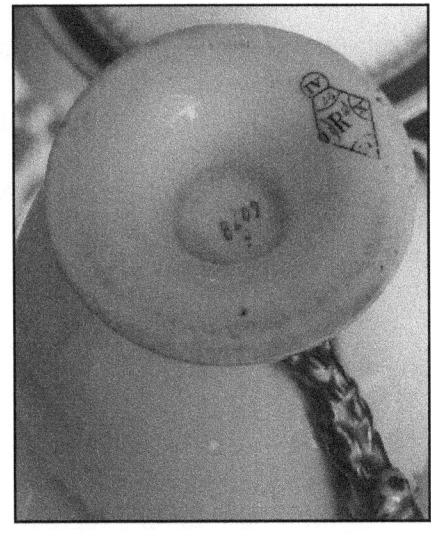

English porcelain tea cup and saucer almost certainly used by Henry Hartley to entertain his wildlife friends with home-grown coffee at his *Thorndale* homestead from 1868

We were able to verify that the *Rd* Registration Mark of the *British Patent Office* on the underside confirms that that teacup is Class IV – on the top of the *Rd* label – (i.e. Class #4 quality English porcelain). The "X" on the right indicates that it was manufactured in 1868. (Not before the 1820 English Settlers arrived in Port Elizabeth, as Cécile's granny had surmised). The exact date of manufacture – by reading the mark – was the 25th of November, 1868 and it came from Kiln Batch #13).[1]

That also accounts for the fact that Cécile only has one surviving tea cup, but THREE remaining saucers from that period of Henry Hartley Family history. The Afrikaner Boers dropped and broke their teacups at *Thorndale* in the process?? Wonderful how we can *read the tea leaves in the bottom of a tea cup*; but then my imagination is getting away from me!!

He also provided them with his own home-grown smoking tobacco products.

Much has been written on Henry Hartley's friendliness and helpfulness to all. He must have also had a keen sense of self-deprecating humour that resonated with everyone he met. Many of his hunting experiences have been repeated around the campfire or coffee table and handed down verbally from one generation to the next.

Imagine relaxing around an open hardwood fire in the bushveld under an African star-lit sky after a long day of hunting wildlife. The sizzle and aroma of roasted kudu fillet and warthog steaks rising above the hot coals makes your mouth water and fill the air. The piercing sound of a fiery-necked nightjar is in the background.

A campfire yarn that does ring true though, is one told by Hartley himself and widely recorded in primary published diaries and notebooks.

The bearded Henry Hunter – looking much older than his young years – would be huddled intensely in front of you, his blue eyes reflected in the flames, enthralling you with the following description of a close encounter he had had with a lion one day . . .

> Frederick, Tom, Willie (his three eldest sons) and I had spent an entire gruelling day tracking a herd of elephant – many with enormous tusks. We had left our horses behind tied to a tree and began stalking them through the thickets on foot. They had not seen or sniffed us. As we approached the grey group quietly feeding in front of us we crouched down to our haunches and stalked them, our guns at the ready to shoot. Suddenly a large

---

[1] We were able to authenticate these heirlooms by consulting a copy of Pears Cyclopedia 87 Edition (1978) – first published in 1897 – (Page U24).

male lion nonchalantly ambled into the clearing between us and the elephants. The King of the Beasts had not seen us. The boys were insistent that I shoot the approaching lion.

"No!" I whispered back in annoyance. I was not going to let an interfering male lion stop us from a very profitable harvest of ivory after such a long hunt.

I went down on all fours and crept closer to the lion from behind a tall termite mound (or low bush by some accounts).[1]

The lion momently halted on the other side of the termite mound. He was not aware of how close he was to me. I slowly and carefully put my head around the termite mound and looked the lion straight in the eye. Without a sound the brute with his majestic golden mane, bolted back in retreat at the unexpected sighting of the long grey beard of a white male hunter.

There was again silence and we were able to stalk within a safe, but comfortable distance, and fire off all four of our large-calibre, 2 bore black-powder elephant guns into the herd.

At his farm in the Magaliesberg, where he kept open house for all travellers, he was known as a liberal entertainer and host.[2]

---

[1] Berrington, Aileen, 1987, p. 191
[2] Le Roux, Servaas. *Pioneers and Sportsmen of South Africa*, 1939, p. 91

Chapter 11:

Medicine man & amateur surgeon in the bush

On one occasion the Ndebele/Zulu King Mzilikazi fractured his arm in several places when he fell off the horse that Hartley had gifted to him as part of his concession payment to hunt wildlife in his Matabele territory. Henry reset and strapped the forearm professionally in splints. It was fully repaired within a few weeks and the Royal Chief was, of course, most grateful. Although Henry was an excellent horseman and marksman, Mzilikazi never did learn to ride a horse or shoot a rifle.

On another occasion, one of Hartley's indunas was up a tree robbing a bee's hive after following a Honey Guide bird to its treasure of honey, "The bees resented the intrusion and stung him so severely that he slipt (sic.) down in a hurry and in so doing he received the blade of an assegai in his arm-pit, the point coming out just below the shoulder".[1] The warrior had ill-advisedly placed his sharp weapon against the stem of the tree before climbing up. Hartley applied a dose of (Epsom) salts for inflammation and tied a piece of cotton cloth around the wound to let it heal.

Almost all explorer/hunters carried a fully stocked medicine chest with them on their journeys into the unknown without qualified doctors around. Thomas Baines, Henry Hartley and Eduard Mohr were particularly proficient in this regard. "Take a dram of quinine dissolved in brandy or spirit before breakfast for fever", Baines recommended.[2] There was often a stream of black Africans appearing at their outspans asking for medicines and treatment. A young child at the Royal Kraal had inserted a glass bead into her ear that became permanently and painfully stuck there. After days of unsuccessful attempts to dislodge the bead, Baines placed some "sweet oil" (olive oil) into the ear. He squirted warm water into the ear using a syringe and the glass bead popped free. Five or six grains of tartar emetic – which induces vomiting – seemed to cure headaches or nausea. Curry powder in warm water while sitting in front of a warm campfire

---

[1] Baines, Thomas, *Diaries of 1869-1872*, edited by Wallis, 1946, p. 467
[2] Baines, Thomas, *Journal of 1877*, pp. 10 & 19

seemed to cure most minor ailments by the following morning! A dose of cayenne pepper was similarly effective. "Cream of Tartar", from the acidic fruit of a baobab tree, was used as a baking powder and cleaning solution. "Carbonate of soda", an alkaline, was used for indigestion. A few drops of opium and a spoonful of sugar was used for snakebites. Chalk and opium for dysentery. Carbonate of ammonia dissolved in warm water and swabbed onto tsetse fly bites seemed to mitigate the effects of deadly sleeping sickness for both humans and domestic animals. The local wildlife was naturally immune to tsetse fly bites.

Henry Hartley and his elder brother by twelve years, Thomas Hartley (Junior) passed down their acquired knowledge of administrating medicines from one generation to the next. I mentioned that Thomas Hartley (Junior) at the age of seventeen, while en route by sailing ship in 1820 from Liverpool to Port Elizabeth (107 days) became the enthusiastic assistant to Dr Calton – the ship's doctor and leader of their immigration party. Thomas (Junior) "showed a special aptitude for and interest in treating the sick". In Bathurst, Thomas (Junior) became the medical comforter, emergency paramedic and extractor of teeth for the community. He also established a very successful pharmacy as part of his general store.[1]

Simon Hartley (b. 1968), a direct descendent from *Rainhill* farm outside Rustenburg in the Magaliesberg mountains has an elder brother Henry Earley Hartley – a practising veterinary surgeon. Their father, Henry Charles Hartley was a very successful pharmacist in Rustenburg for all his life. Henry Charles was Deputy Mayor of Rustenburg twice in the 1970s and very active in the community. He died while on holiday in Sweden of an unexpected heart attack at the age of 88 on April 20, 2020. This was on the night before he was due to fly home to South Africa at the start of severe international travel lockdowns imposed worldwide by the reaction to the Covid-19 pandemic.

---

[1] Berrington, Aileen, 1987, p. 24

Chapter 12:

An oft-told tale of Henry Hartley discovering the Victoria Falls BEFORE David Livingstone

As with most legendary figures, many false myths follow them into perpetuity. One such myth is that Henry "discovered" the Victoria Falls no later than 1849 in the company of Frederick, his three or four-year eldest son, and six years before Dr David Livingstone. Why would anyone want to take their first-born toddler on such a perilous exploratory expedition into unknown darkest Africa?

The Zambezi River Valley was widely known, even then, as a low-lying fever-infested, rock-strewn, desert-like terrain with almost no potable drinking water, and no ox-wagon access. It could only be accessed on foot with great difficulty. Reading David Livingstone's, Eduard Mohr's, Thomas Leask's, and Thomas Baines's diaries on trying to reach the magnificent spectacle attests to these challenging hurdles.

Henry Hartley was much more interested in following the spoor of elephants and looking for quartz-bearing gold reefs, than he was in visiting a waterfall in the deadly, insect-infested Zambezi River Gorge. There is no evidence that Henry Hartley even came within 150 miles of the Zambezi River.[1] He preferred the "Old Hunter's Road" at higher elevations that he pioneered himself, which was free of tsetse fly, up to Hartley and Hartley Hills, nearer to the future Salisbury.

Henry may have been a modest fellow, but was not shy in bragging about his legendary elephant hunting skills, or being a trusted confidant to both Chief Mzilikazi and his successor and son Chief Lobengula at the Royal Kraal near Bulawayo. Neither was he shy about rediscovering ancient gold mining workings, and being the first white man to travel as far north as the Umvusi River and the headwaters of the Sabi River in 1867, in the central part of the future Zimbabwe. Hartley never claimed to have visited the Victoria Falls.

In July 1938, a Captain Reginald "Hartley" Thackeray, who claims Henry Hartley as his famous maternal grandfather, perpetuates the

---

[1] Le Roux, *Pioneers and Sportsmen of South Africa*, 1939, p. 90

false myth that Henry Hartley "discovered" the stupendous cataract before David Livingstone in November 1858.[1]

I found at least a dozen-and-a-half factual errors in Captain Thackeray's published journal article. That mythical Hartley family fable is also recorded in Berrington[2] as having been verbally passed on by Henry Hartley's Hottentot (mixed-race) wagon driver, named Cresjan.

A few tabloid press articles repeat the myth: *The Sunday Times* of Johannesburg in November 1936, and an article entitled "Eeerste by Victoria?" written by S Vercuell, and published in *Die Burger* on December 4, 1976, as well as a so-called personal diary of Henry Hartley's *In sy groot dagboek het hy deeglike beskrywings van die diere en plante van die omgewing gegee.* The diary does not exist.

Like watching *CNN* and *Fox News* today, the *Die Burger* article is, in my opinion, just slanted misinformation and exaggerated, unsubstantiated conjecture. I wish I was wrong.

My information is that Henry Hartley only arrived by ox-wagon at Potchefstroom around 1845, and to *Thorndale* farm in the Magaliesberg in 1846. He would not have had an opportunity to discover Victoria Falls at the same time as re-establishing himself as a young father, as a farmer (introducing tobacco and citrus) and a big-game hunter in the far north-eastern Transvaal.

The number of elephants that Hartley killed during his professional hunting career is also probably exaggerated speculation. Numbers vary from 500 to 1,000 to over 2,000 dead elephants, depending on who is telling the story.

Dr David Livingstone was the first European Explorer to "rediscover" the renamed Victoria Falls on November 17, 1855. Hartley's first hunting trip north to that part of southern Africa (probably to Bechuanaland) was only around 1861, FIVE years later, and much later as far north as Chief Mzilikazi's kraal near Bulawayo, who strictly controlled access to his territory. This was SIX years later than Dr Livingstone's "discovery" of that phenomenal spectacle, which was well reported in the authoritative geographic journals at the time. Like Thomas Baines of the same era, David Livingstone was pedantic and methodical in his recording of accurate facts – including his first transcontinental walking exploratory journey right across Africa from the Portuguese-controlled port of Luanda on the west coast, along the Zambezi River Valley all the way to the Indian ocean mouth

---

[1] Captain Reginald "Hartley" Thackeray in an article published by the Royal African Society entitled *"Henry Hartley – African Hunter and Explorer"* in July 1938, pp. 283-297
[2] Berrington, Aileen, 1987, p. 191

of the Zambezi River on the Portuguese-controlled east coast at the river port of Senna.

Livingstone renamed these world-famous falls the **Victoria Falls** after his British Queen Victoria. At the time they were known as *The Smoke that Thunders* or "Mosi-oa-Tunya" by the local Batonga tribe.

David Livingstone was personally known to Thomas Baines who would have accompanied the famous London Missionary Society Explorer as an artist and scientific geographer on his transcontinental trip starting from Luanda, if it were not for a falling out with David Livingstone's brother, Charles Livingstone in 1858, because of logistical and financial disagreements.[1]

Thomas Baines did himself travel with James Chapman on his expedition to the Victoria Falls in 1861 from Walvis Bay on the west coast of south-west Africa across the Namib desert German Protectorate to Lake Ngami in the British-controlled Kalahari hinterland and then along the Chobe River to the Victoria Falls before returning to Pietermaritzburg in the Natal Colony of South Africa.

On this occasion Thomas Baines was able to make numerous sketches and oil paintings of his trip to the Victoria Falls and its

[1] Baines, Thomas, *Journal of 1877*, p. xiv

Thomas Baines and James Chapman in a dugout canoe going to view Victoria Falls on August 13, 1862 painted by Thomas Baines on November 9, 1863 (Zimbabwe Archives)

spectacular scenery, which became widely distributed through King George and the Royal Geographic Society.

Fellow travellers to the falls, Thomas Baines and James Chapman, are shown in the dugout canoe with brown beards. Henry Hartley wore a long silver beard at that time, and is not depicted in this iconic painting.

Captain Reginald Thackery's 1938 unsubstantiated utterings of his family claim are highly speculative and circumstantial at the least.

At least six explorers in that historic period – Mohr, Thomas Baines, Leask, Mauch, Lee, and Livingstone himself – travelled with Henry Hartley at various times, kept detailed notes of their interactions and had their diaries published. Not one of them mentioned that Henry Hartley had even attempted to reach the Victoria Falls. Neither did Henry.

In a burst of false propaganda, the Hon. P.K. van der Byl, MP for Hartley District, boasted that Henry Hartley discovered the Victoria Falls before David Livingstone in 1855! This was at the unveiling ceremony of bronze plaques on the 100th anniversary of the establishment of the settlement at Hartley Hill on September 28, 1969. Van der Byl was Minister of Information, Immigration and Tourism at the time in Ian Smith's Rhodesian Front government. There is no foundation to that claim.

Even as recently as 2020, in published books and articles, commentators perpetuate this historical misinformation – relying heavily on Captain Thackeray's 1938 erroneous secondary sources.

Being a famous 1800's elephant hunter and southern African explorer there is so much conjecture out there on Henry Hartley. The myth continues today.

Chapter 13:

The fearless elephant hunter

It is highly likely that Henry Hartley started hunting elephants and other valuable wildlife in the eastern Cape in his youth, until they became almost extinct in that area. He moved up to the Transvaal around 1841 as an ox-wagon trader between Grahamstown, Potchefstroom, and Rustenburg, and established his *Thorndale* farm in the Magaliesberg. He is believed to have been hunting in the north-eastern parts of the Transvaal as early as 1845. He went further north across the Limpopo River in 1861, and also as far east as Lake Ngami in the Kalahari desert, near Mtewetwe Salt Pan, where his hunting party was affected with small pox in that year.[1] His highly lucrative hunting trips continued in more earnest in the direction of western Matabeleland around 1865.

His three sons, Frederick, Tom and William later played a prominent part in his dangerous, but highly lucrative, hunting expeditions from their teenage years, as did his stepson Tom Maloney – from his third marriage.

The total tally of dead elephants that Henry Hartley was purportedly personally responsible for has been more narrowly estimated at 1,000 to 1,200 by most sources. It is probably an exaggeration over the duration of his professional hunting career. A personal record of 1,200 dead elephants would make him the highest killer of elephants in the world.[2]

According to Berrington,[3] the Reverend Arthur J. Chaplin, one-time Rector of Fort Beaufort, put together an unpublished biographical "pamphlet" on the life of his father-in-law, Henry Hartley, also claiming that Hartley had killed in excess of 1,200 elephants. I have not been able to track down that "pamphlet", nor any purported diaries in the hand of Henry Hartley himself which, sadly, either do not exist, or were lost in arson fires set by British Imperial forces at *Thorndale* farm and on a Hartley family's farm in Vryburg during the Anglo-Boer War of 1899-1902.

---

[1] Le Roux, 1939, p. 89
[2] It is possible that another Boer hunter by the name of Petrus Jacobs may hold that infamous record (p. 91, Le Roux).
[3] Berrington, Aileen, 1987, p. 195

Thousands of elephants were slaughtered each year in the mid 1800s in the far northern ZAR Transvaal Republiek. The Voortrekker village of Zoutpansbergdorp (Schoemansdal) was a major marketing location for selling ivory to merchants from the Cape, Natal and nearby Moçambique. "In 1864, one merchant alone shipped out 312 cwts. (1 cwt.= 100 pounds weight), the product of 350 animals". Even at 14 shillings, 7 pence per pound of ivory that would amount to a very considerable amount in British Sterling.[1]

A Hartley relative does mention that he did in one good season in 1865 earn "39,000 pounds of animal product". It is not known whether that figure was in £ sterling, or in weight? On another occasion in a letter on June 3, 1867 written by Mrs Thomas Hartley (Junior) – the spouse of the elder brother of Henry – writes that Henry had "last season a splendid hunt the produce of which brought in 15,000 pounds, if only half that sum it was a great deal".[2]

Notwithstanding that Mzilikazi was paralyzed and on his deathbed in 1868 he did allow Henry Hartley to again take in a hunting party that season. They bagged 160 elephants and passed through the Royal Kraal on September 5, 1868 for the customary pot of beer on exiting the Matabele kingdom.[3]

Hartley certainly had excellent ivory hunts in both the 1869 and 1870 winter hunting seasons around Hartley Hills, as chronicled by Eduard Mohr, Thomas Leask and Thomas Baines in their diaries.

No doubt he killed several hundred elephant and other valuable wildlife, in the highly lucrative ivory trade when an abundance of elephant roamed the north.

Environmental protectionism was not a consideration in the north, but Transvaal Republic President Paul Kruger is credited with preserving wildlife in the north-eastern lowveld parts of South Africa within the tsetse fly belt for posterity. The world-renowned *Kruger National Park* still bears his name – one of the largest game reserves in the world.

While Henry Hartley and his white English and Afrikaner Boer hunters were decimating the African elephants and rhinos in Matabeleland in their thousands for their tusks in the 1860s and 1870s, the American white pioneers were slaughtering Bison Buffalo in the their millions across the vast prairies of North America to starve the American native Indians of their main food source.

---

[1] Bulpin, T.V., *Lost Trails of the Transvaal*, 3rd Edition 1974, pp. 106 & 117
[2] Berrington, Aileen, 1987, p. 30, probably referring to the 1866 hunting season.
[3] From *The Story of Hartley Hills* by J.A. Bowen on the occasion of the 100th anniversary celebration of Hartley Hill town.

Today the disorganized governments of Zimbabwe and Mozambique continue to allow corrupt hunting practices of the remaining elephant and rhino populations within their territories. With genetic evolution there is more likelihood that elephants will be born "tuskless". Hundreds of thousands of elephants in Kenya and Tanzania were slaughtered for their ivory during the 1960s and 1970s. Ninety percent of the remaining wild elephants in Mozambique were slaughtered by both warring Frelimo and Renamo factions during the civil wars between 1977 and 1992. 18.5% of female Mozambique elephants were tuskless before the civil war. That proportion has risen to 33% today.[1]

---

[1] BBC World News, October 22, 2021

Chapter 14:

Trampled by a charging white rhinoceros

Whatever actually happened on Friday, November 26, 1869,[1] en route back from an ivory hunting and gold quartz exploration trip, can only be deduced from the various tellings of the same incident by different authors.

That it was a near fatal accident for Henry Hartley is no doubt true. The stories all contribute to the mythology of this legendary big-game hunter.

> The most accurate version, in my opinion, is that recorded by Thomas Baines (his travelling companion and good friend from 1869 to 1875) in his diary on that unfortunate date. The diary entry reads . . . "My friend Mr. Hartley has met with a sad accident. He had dismounted to shoot a rhinoceros and, seeing it fall, had gone up to it before it was dead. His lameness prevented his escape and he was tossed by the nose of the huge animal, thrown upon its back and, I believe, trampled on. The shouts of his Hottentot[2] scared the beast away and the boy then made for the waggons at Ramaqueban. The remainder of the party of course saddled up and while some hastened to his assistance, others rode to Tati to fetch the Doctor who fortunately was at hand, and, returning with them reached the waggons almost as soon as the sufferer was brought there. It appeared that he had two ribs broken, besides other injuries, but was considered to be recovering and was soon after removed to Tati".[3]

Published diary versions by Thomas Leask (1870), Eduard Mohr (1876), and John Lee (1877) all corroborate this account of events.

Tati, forty-four miles southwards, was the location of gold mine diggings at present-day Francistown in neighbouring Bechuanaland (present-day Botswana).

---

[1] Mohr, Eduard. 1876, p. 202, corroborates the date and the circumstances of that almost-fatal trampling.
[2] His devoted, life-long hunting companion of mixed race, born in the Cape Colony.
[3] Baines, Thomas, *Diaries of 1869–1872*, edited by Wallis, 1946, p. 230

Hartley had a painful ride on a jolting ox-cart to Tati, where "Dr Coverley pronounced his recovery certain, but ordered absolute rest for six weeks".[1]

Following the able care of the Edinburgh-educated doctor, Hartley returned by ox-wagon to his farm *Thorndale* in the Magaliesberg for full rest and recuperation.

He was up and about again and fit enough the following June to August 1870 to ride his horse 800 miles back to Hartley Hills with two heavily-laden ox-wagons to trade, and to enthusiastically hunt elephants and other valuable big-game again. He rejoined his hunting party which included his sons Frederick, Thomas and Willie, and stepson Tom Maloney.

The most exaggerated version of the rhino charge is that told by Crejan[2] and handed from one generation to the next by Hartley family descendants. The story grows more "legs, arms and other exaggerated appendages" with each subsequent telling. The further away in time from the incident the more "Wow!" the story becomes. Part of the embellishment may have originated from Henry Hartley himself!? The hunter was well known for entertaining his guests with stories of his exploits around a campfire.

Is this what recording historic facts is all about? We add bits of information that never happened merely to suit the narrative and biases that we hold. We leave out vital pieces of information. The reader is none the wiser.

The versions published by Captain Reginald "Hartley" Thackeray (1939), Charles Henry Hartley (1976), Aileen Berrington (1987), and others, appear to be based on earlier anecdotal information and conjecture, without checking for authenticity or cross-examination of the historic facts, geography, or the reasonableness of their assumptions.

The most embellished version is that repeated by Aileen Berrington as told by Henry Hartley's devoted "Hottentot" ox-wagon driver, Crejan . . .

> Many tales have been handed down about this almost legendary figure: . . . Henry was walking with his horse following, when a rhino suddenly charged. He shot and mortally wounded the rhino when it was only a few paces from him. The rhino overtook him and tossed him into the air. He came down on the beast's back only narrowly avoiding the terrible horns. Unfor-

---

[1] Mohr, Eduard. 1876, p. 203

[2] Crejan was Henry Hartley's "Hottentot" (mixed-race) ox-wagon driver and hunting assistant.

tunately, the rhino in his death throes rolled over onto him and collapsed, dead, pinning him down, only his hands and the top part of his body being free. Henry's horse Bokkie, was an old friend and over the years there had developed a close communion between him and his master, which now stood Henry in good stead. Calling Bokkie, he commanded him to lie down in such a way that he could get hold of the stirrup. Bokkie then pulled him from under the rhino. Henry then let go of the stirrup, and commanded the horse: "Camp, Bokkie, camp!" and the horse returned to camp and led members of the rescue party back. Henry was seriously injured and never quite recovered. He died from his injuries two years later, and was buried on his farm *Thorndale*.[1]

This version of the incident is flamboyant, grossly exaggerated, and far from the truth. Why would he need his horse, Bokkie, to pull him free when he had a "Hottentot" assistant with his own horse? Crejan would almost certainly also have had his own two-bore elephant gun with him at the scene? Unlike most other "lazy" European hunters (including Thomas Baines, Eduard Mohr and Thomas Leask) who allowed servants to carry their heavy hunting rifles following behind them, Henry was always on horseback because of his foot disability, and always carried his own gun while riding to shoot game, even from the saddle if the opportunity suddenly arose.

Henry did not die two years later, but died **seven years later**, after fully recovering and going back north to hunt yet again almost as actively as he had done in the past, the very next winter hunting season of 1870.

He still had plenty of energy to weld (forge) a wagon wheel rim for fellow hunter Thomas Leask on the day he arrived back at the Hartley Hills hunting camp on August 20, 1870. This was the same day that he learnt of his son Willie's premature death from black-water fever for the very first time, AND was able to chase after and shoot five elephants on horseback just a few days later together with his party of hunters on their way to view the gravesite, 22 miles away.[2]

This reminds me of Nobel Literature Prize winning author J.M. Coetzee's famous idiom . . . "All fictional writing is autobiographical, and all autobiography is fiction".

While riding out to visit the grave of Willie Hartley, Henry and his hunting party suddenly came across the spoor of a herd of eleven bull

---

[1] Berrington, Aileen, 1987, p. 191
[2] Baines, Thomas, *Diaries of 1869–1872*, edited by Wallis, 1946, p. 454; and Leask, Thomas, *Southern African Diaries of 1865–1870*, edited by Wallis, 1954, p. 212

elephants, most with huge tusks, grazing nearby. The startled elephants moved forward with a shuffling "walk". Elephants can initially outrun a horse through the thick bush, but they tire easily within a short distance. Hartley in his enthusiasm for more ivory immediately gave orders for a chase.[1]

> "Oude Baas" was to the front at once and Jewell and I fell just so far back as to leave the professional hunters unobstructed, while we kept close up, to observe and follow their movements. We dipped into a little spruit, crossed it in the thick grass and, as we came out, saw the sterns of the herd in full flight. The hunters formed line-abreast and started in chase. I gave my horse the rein too freely and, having once felt his liberty, he took the full advantage of it and would not acknowledge a check. My hat came off and, falling before my face, blinded me for the moment, during which I lost hold of my gun, and when I shook my hat clear, I was rushing through a dense but fortunately narrow belt of *Matchabeela* trees and saplings in hot pursuit of Klaas, Mr. Hartley's little Hottentot, who's [sic] horse, less impetuous than mine, or checked in his career by a young thicket, received the full shock of mine upon his quarter, the collision throwing me forward, while a tree behind caught and tore away my off-stirrup, at the same time dragging the saddle (the girth's of which were loose with so many hours riding) so far back that it turned over with me.

The force of the collision threw Thomas Baines off his mount and he had to give up the chase, without his hat or his gun. The chase was too much for his horse, *Dutchman*, who unexpectedly died that night.

After elephants run out of initial "steam" they need to pause to recover their flight energy. The typical strategy of the hunters was to outflank them on the one side and chase ahead, then turn their horses into the fleeing elephant herd and shoot at them from the broadside and into the shoulder where the heavy elephant rifles loaded with six-to-the-pound lead slugs that could penetrate into the heart and drop the animal almost immediately.[2]

---

[1] Baines, Thomas, *Diaries of 1869–1872*, edited by Wallis, 1946, p. 454; and Leask, Thomas, *Southern African Diaries of 1865–1870*, edited by Wallis, 1954, p. 212

[2] "Despite their enormous power, the short low-velocity slugs still suffered the penetration issues which plagued guns of this era, particularly for the toughest shot of all: defeating the bone mass for a frontal brain shot on an elephant. Thus, dangerous game hunting in the 19th century was as much a test of the gun-bearer's ability to relay guns to the hunter, and of horsemanship to evade charges long enough to reload". (Source Fadala, Sam, *They were after ivory*, Wisonsin)

On this occasion five elephants had been killed, of which two were shot by Hartley himself. A lucrative hunt.

Henry Hartley became affectionally known by everyone, including the Matabele, as "Ou Baas", or "Ouda Baas".[1]

The rough pencil sketch[2] shown below, drawn by Thomas Baines of a dead white rhinoceros – and vulture (Erona) – in his field notebook is not the same rhinoceros that nearly killed Henry Hartley a month later. It is more likely that Thomas Baines shot this particular white rhinoceros himself – mentioned in his Journal around the same time. Baines also makes no mention of Henry Hartley suffering any serious

[1] Old master or grandfather.
[2] Baines, Thomas, Papers. Original Field Notes of September 20, 1869. MS.049.9.3 (p. 56). The Brenthurst Library, Johannesburg

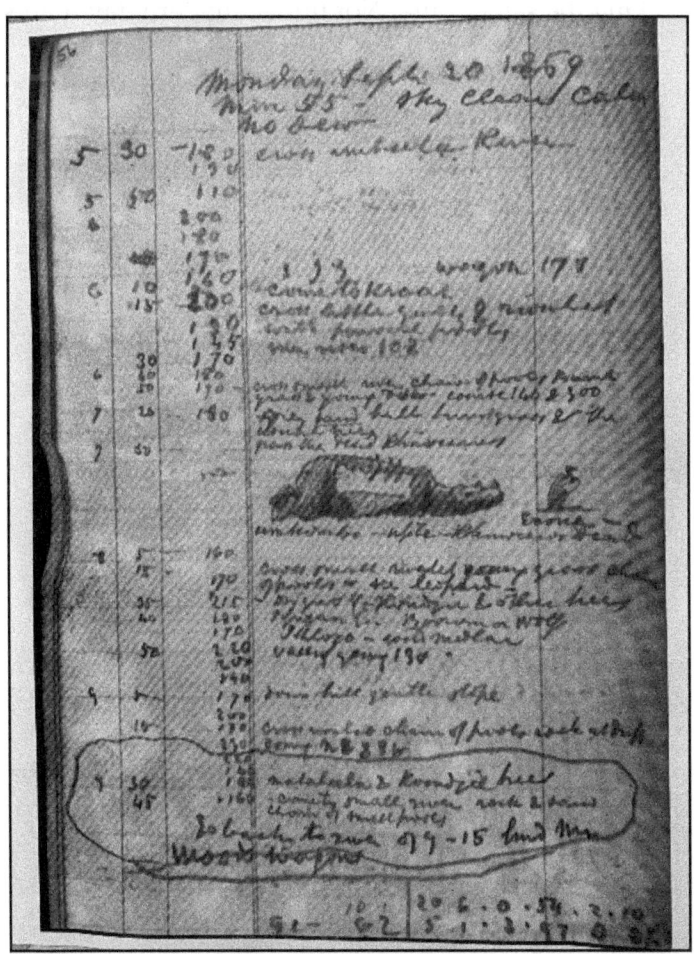

Extract from Thomas Baines's original field notebook for Monday September 20, 1869

injury from this particular dead white rhinoceros in adjoining pages of his diary or original field notes.

Rhino were also in high demand for their horns, tough thick hide for making leather sandals and ample venison. The diarist adventurers of the time record numerous instances of shooting these slow-moving, but potentially highly aggressive and dangerous giants.

The sketch is interesting in that it also includes other information that Baines recorded every day, such as the weather, measurement in yards travelled and magnetic compass direction taken; and his calculations for average latitude in degrees, minutes and seconds observed, plus altitude determined from the boiling point of water. He would often carve the latitude position on the bark of a prominent tree at each overnight outspan for the benefit of other fellow adventures trekking the same route. Not unlike modern day road signs.

A pencil drawing of a hunter shooting an elephant (provided by Michael Tucker) from a sketch that he photographed at the National Archives of Rhodesia.
Note that the "hunter's horse is trained to stand with loose reins and forelegs braced against the shock of the discharge"

Henry Hartley in middle-age
(from Thomas Leask's diary p. 307)

Chapter 15:

Character & physical description as a mature adult

Henry Hartley was a handsome man with blond hair and grey-blue eyes in his youth. Despite the physical disability from birth to his feet he had a superb physique. He became an **expert horse rider and marksman**. He was known for his **astute mind, multi-linguism, bravery, entrepreneurship, innovation, generosity and kindness to others.** These talents and character attributes are expanded on elsewhere in this biography. He chose to grow his beard out to shoulder length as a middle aged adult. This disguised his age, and he walked with a limp owing to a club foot.

A fellow explorer/hunter Eduard Mohr states in his diary that Henry Hartley was an old man of **seventy-two** years when he met him for the first time on June 11, 1869, because he had a "long silver beard"; "has been an elephant hunter since his twenty-sixth year, and is well known from Potchefstroom to the Zambezi"; "had shot altogether over one thousand elephants" in his hunting career; is "at present the oldest and greatest hunter of Africa south of the Zambezi", "was muscular, well-tanned by the sun, and walked with a limp: and was charged and badly injured by a white rhinoceros as he shot it dead two weeks later".[1]

Henry Hartley was in fact only *fifty-four* years old at the time. A discrepancy of **eighteen years**!

Strange. We know that Hartley had a **keen sense of humour** and was a practical joker. I can imagine that the source of that "misinformation" may well have come from Hartley himself!

It was not only secondary sources, but even primary sources (such as Mohr, who had actually met Hartley in the flesh and travelled with him in 1869 and 1870) who spread false information and made mistakes with the historic facts.

How could Mohr, as a perfectionist German astronomer/trader/hunter/explorer/zoologist make such an error of judgment and record it? Mohr was the first German explorer to visit the Victoria Falls. He did so by walking ±350 miles from the Tati gold diggings

---

[1] Mohr, Eduard, 1876, pp. 121 & 202. An accomplished astronomer, but not astute enough to determine the approximate age of a man he met face-to-face.

through desert-like, hilly savannah bush having almost no potable water and took three months to reach the famous cataracts.

Notwithstanding that he was a professional hunter Henry Hartley showed **emotion** in identifying with the pain suffered, in particular by giraffes, who had been shot and injured, but not immediately killed. It was the typical hunters' *modus operandi* to drive the wounded animal towards the wagons to be slaughtered there, so that their very heavy carcases, and about five metres of height, did not have to be loaded onto an additional ox-wagon for transport to camp to be skinned and butchered. Giraffes would frequently shed tears in terror of imminent death. "Mr. Hartley says the pitiful sight has often moved him to kill the poor creature at once rather than prolong its agony by driving it farther", writes Thomas Baines.[1]

On another occasion a lion had taken down and killed a large bull eland antelope by suffocating and holding on to its neck. The lion was trying to drag his prize away on its back. But the lion had overrated his own strength. Hartley watched as the lion's hind legs slipped from under him and collapsed, with the full weight of the dying eland pinning him down on his belly. He found the two animals in this position with the lion barely alive: The weight of the eland on top, with the lion's teeth still firmly embedded in the neck of the eland. Hartley shot the lion to put it out of his misery, and became the owner of both predator and prey. A mature male eland can be as big as a moose, weigh between 400 and 1,000kg, and stand 1.8m in height at the shoulder. Biltong made from eland venison was highly prized by the hunters, and the black tribesmen believed that lion venison would impart strength in battle.[2]

Jane Carruthers[3] was able to confirm two additional character traits that I had been exploring on Henry Hartley: his **"modesty"**, adding **"Diplomat Extraordinaire"** to his many talents.[4]

Geologist Herr Karl Mauch was indignant that it was he and not Henry Hartley who should take credit for discovering old tribal gold diggings at Hartley Hills. Thomas Baines set the public record straight by concluding that while "Mr. Hartley saw the diggings and of course, connected them with the legends . . . He never pretended to be a scientific explorer, that is the honourable share due to Herr

---

[1] Baines, Thomas, *Diaries of 1869–1872, Baines Goldfields Diaries* on July 26, 1871, edited by Wallis, 1946, p. 651). The leather from the giraffe's neck and along its thighs was often spliced together and used as strong rope to pull heavy ox-wagons

[2] Leask, Thomas, *Southern African Diaries of 1865–1870*, edited by Wallis, 1954, p. 86

[3] Emeritus Professor of History at the University of South Africa, in an article entitled *Fredrich Jeppe: Mapping the Transvaal c. 1850-1899*, 2003, p. 967

[4] from her article on the "Early Boer Republics changing political forces . . .": *A Search for Origins ...* , 2007, p. 196

Mauch"[1] . . . "The honour of first discovery is properly attributable to Hartley", and confirmed to be gold by Mauch.

Especially in the early days of the Boer Republics, "the Voortrekkers were suspicious to a paranoid degree of all visitors and particularly of anyone who was English-speaking, because they were so afraid of losing their independence, as had happened to them in Natal".[2] Hartley, an 1820 English Settler, but already a land owner and citizen of the Transvaal Republiek when he settled on his *Thorndale* Magaliesberg farm in the early 1840s, was arrested at Ohrigstad in 1846 on his way to hunt in the Soutpansberg (in the far northeastern Transvaal) "despite having a letter of introduction from his local commandant, Gerrit Kruger, that allowed him to trade as far

---

[1] Baines, Thomas, *Diaries of 1869–1872*, edited by Wallis, 1946, p. 616
[2] Carruthers, Jane, Chapter 11, *A Search for Origins*, 2007, p. 196, referencing Transvaal Archives TAB SSO R114/46

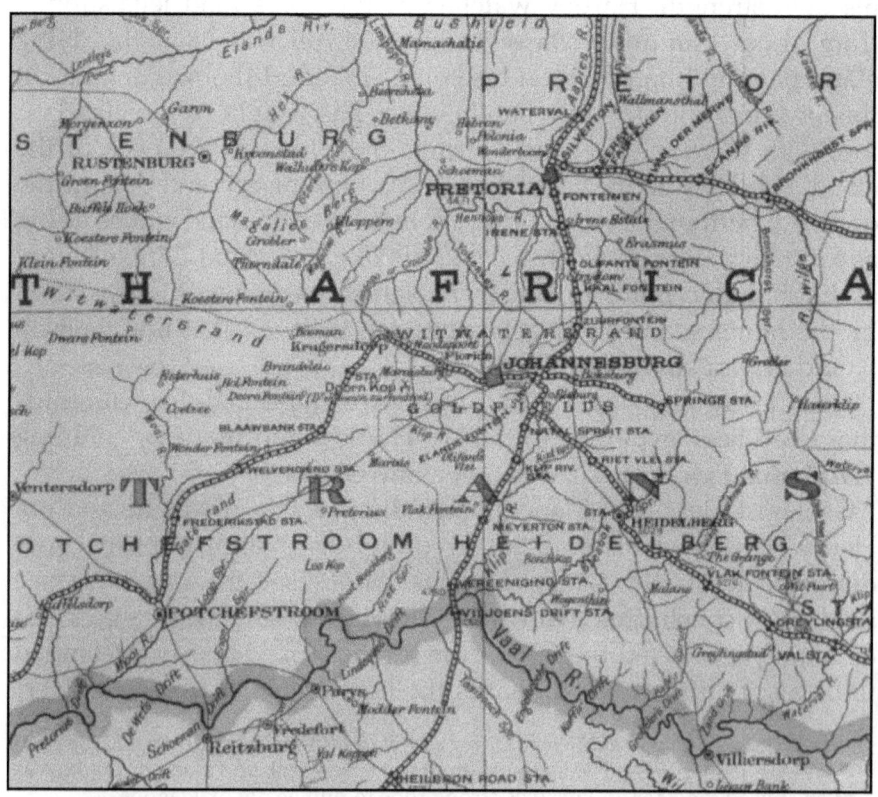

Map of the OFS and ZAR Transvaal Republics, before the Second Anglo-Boer War in 1899, published by Edward Stanford, London, showing location of *Thorndale* farm

north as the Olifants River. Thomas Baines, too, was detained at Potchefstroom in 1850 for carrying a sextant!

Almost all of those pre-1899 locations are shown on the attached Map – purchased from *Barry Lawrence Rare Maps*.

It also indicates place names of towns and cities that were until recently known as Port Elizabeth, East London, King Williamstown, Grahamstown and Uitenhage in the Eastern Cape. Algoa Bay has, for the last twenty years, been known as Nelson Mandela Bay. For the previous 400 years it was known by its original name. The Portuguese explorer Bartolomeu Dias was the first European mariner to reach Algoa Bay in 1488.

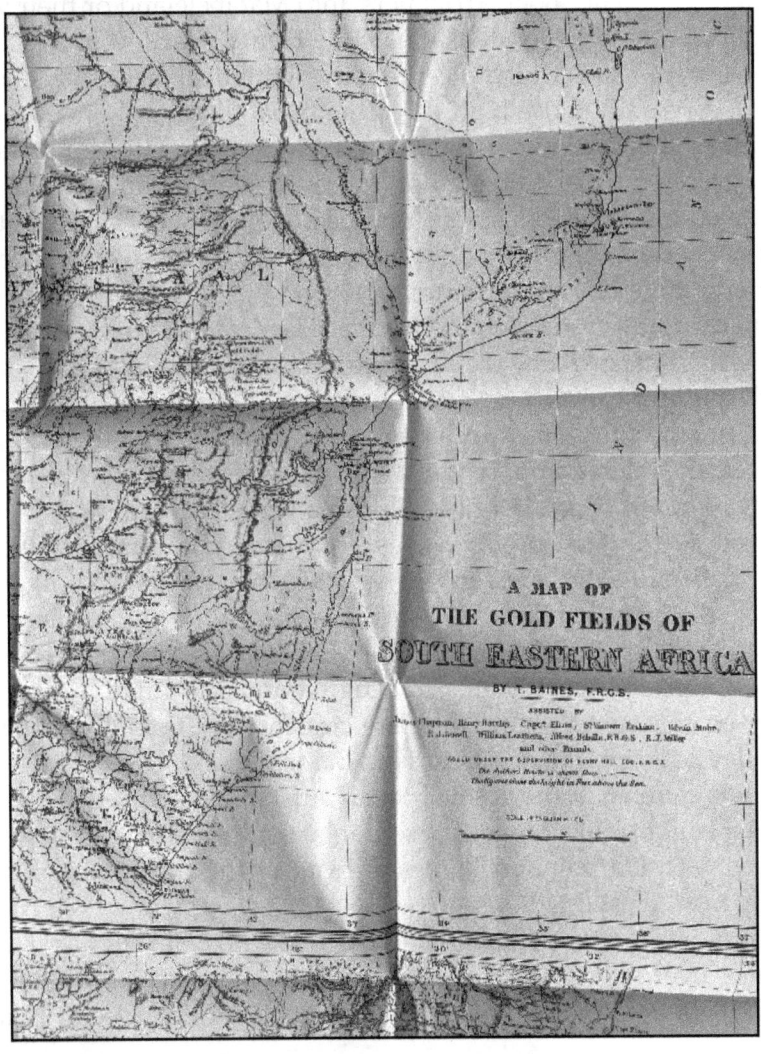

Map of Southern Africa prepared from Thomas Baines' Journals in 1871 showing location of *Thorndale* farm and Hartley outpost

Henry Hartley was a brave and fearless individual whether he was up close to a charging elephant, rhino or lion, or whether he was in imminent danger of personal attack by a mob of delinquent tribesmen trying to steal something of value from his ox-wagon train.[1] He was an **extraordinary diplomat** in dealing with Ndebele/Zulu Kings and lesser local chieftains. **He fully understood pre-colonial Matabele "etiquette"**. Thomas Baines learned much from him. Hartley was loyal and trusted by his friends and acquaintances in business dealings, irrespective of the colour of their skin or hierarchy in their societies.

Mzilikazi and Lobengula were always suspicious about white intruders, especially Boer Afrikaners, into Matabeleland or their vassal neighbouring state of Mashonaland. Henry Hartley and Thomas Baines were respectful and cooperative with the blacks they encountered, especially those high up in the tribal hierarchy, such as Chief Mzilikazi, his interim regent between reigns, Elder Um Nombata, and his successor Chief Lobengula. But, even Hartley and Baines were followed by indunas or spies from the Royal Kraal to ensure that they did not exceed their respective verbal hunting license or prospecting permit granted by the bantu tribal King.

There is considerable evidence that Hartley and Baines took great pains in understanding their culture, language, and hierarchy – albeit with the profit motive in mind for ivory hunting and diamond and gold prospecting. They understood, for instance, that the eldest son Kuruman and heir apparent of Mzilikazi's chief wife, Xwalile, (seemingly born out of adultery to a Shangaan chief, according to Mzilikazi) was not his first preference as a successor, but that his favourite son, Lobengula, by a lesser wife was his choice. Mzilikazi had all of that side of the Royal family murdered, except for the primary wife, Xwalile, who was obligated to adopt Lobengula as her own child and groom him for succession. "Lobengula and Kuruman are brothers only on the father's side; they are cousins on the mother's (side)", Hartley had to explain to his friend Baines.[2]

While camped in the open air at an outspan on their treks on a cool winter's night, even the lowest servants would be invited to take their places with Hartley and Baines in front of the warm campfire and away from prowling lions.

There is no record that I can find of Henry Hartley, or Thomas Baines, ever killing any person – not even during the Frontier Wars in the eastern Cape Colony. Henry Hartley was also wise in "reading

---

[1] Thackeray, 1939 and Berrington, 1987
[2] Baines's *Northern Goldfields* Diaries, for August 30, 1871, edited by Wallis, 1946. pp. 623 & 701

the tea leaves" of a situation: In a request from the Transvaal Republiek for Hartley to act as agent/ambassador for them in their dealings with the Matabele sovereignty, which Hartley refrained from doing, Chief Lobengula was equally wise. He preferred to have good relations with the Lieutenant Governor of the Natal Colony, Sir Theophiles Shepstone, representing the British Queen Victoria rather than the Afrikaner Boers led by President Andries Pretorius at the time. He also had a letter written to the Consul General of Portugal in South Africa instructing the Portuguese settlers to keep out of his territory.

In July 1871 when Henry Hartley did not accompany Thomas Baines to the Royal Kraal, Lobengula had an additional personal letter addressed to his trusted friend Henry Hartley "reprimanding" him for not coming up to visit him in his Royal Kraal on that occasion, and jokingly added in a postscript that he would give his good English friend a hiding with a sjambok (a leather whip used by the natives, Boers and English settlers for corporal punishment) the next time he visited. Such was the trust between the Warrior King of the Matabele nation and Henry Hartley in influencing political affairs in the region.

Corporal punishment in British school settings was the norm in the Victorian era.

With his diplomatic flair Hartley, nevertheless, showed the way for Afrikaner Boer hunters to negotiate successfully with the Ndebele/Zulu warriors for hunting and prospecting licences in the 1860s. By the 1870s there was a plethora of white European hunters and mineral prospectors prowling around Matabeleland and the adjoining Ndebele/Zulu-controlled Mashonaland. Its riches were beginning to be noticed by none other than Cecil John Rhodes of Kimberley Diamond mines fame, whose imperialist vision was to build a railway line from Cape Town to Cairo and colonise the territories along the entire route for the British Empire. Henry Hartley, perhaps unknowingly, paved the way for the eventual overthrow and defeat of the Matabele by the British Imperialist Cecil John Rhodes, and his chief implementor Dr Jameson and the 100-man Rhodesian Pioneer Column at Bulawayo in the early 1890s. They used deadly, just-invented, Maxim machine guns against primitive weapons, long after Henry Hartley was buried. The tribesmen fatally believed that the rapid-fire bullets could not injure them, and they would be protected from harm by their large Zulu animal shields and *muti* (witch-doctor's medicine). Thus Rhodesia came under total British control by 1894. British colonization began in earnest and only ceased with firstly the Unilateral Declaration of Independence by the minority white Ian

Smith regimé on November 11, 1965, and then full independence won by the majority Robert Mugabe ZANU-PF Liberation Army supported by Chinese and Soviet interveners in 1980. Mugabe was a member of the Mashona ethnic group.

The animosity between the Matabele and Mashona peoples continued unabated more than a century later, well after final independence from British colonialism and Ian Smith minority rule in 1980.

Joshua Nkomo, a Matabele from Bulawayo, who came second in the national elections of 1980 wanted to have power.

Robert Mugabe, a Mashona from Salisbury (now Harare) and winner in the elections wanted to have exclusive power.

It was only after a further thirty years of increasingly despotic rule and the death of Mugabe at the age of 95 in 2019 that his veteran lieutenant in the liberation struggle, Emmerson Mnangagwa, known as the "Crocodile" effectively took over. The country is a failed State.

Chapter 16:

Advisor and confidant to Ndebele/Zulu King Mzilikazi and his successor Chief Lobengula

The Matabele nation and paramount chief insisted that any European trader, hunter or prospector, given permission to come into his kingdom, use a loyal Matabele induna as his official guide. The trader was required to feed, accommodate and pay the induna for his services, usually in the form of glass beads (white glass beads, not blue glass beads?) and a hunting rifle with a small lead bar to make bullets and a quantity of gun powder. Such remuneration was held in trust by the chief and then presented to the Induna on successful completion of the contract.

Hunting rifles were, of course, in high demand, but the warrior tribesmen were not very good marksmen and did not get much practice in handling or shooting a sophisticated breech-loading gun. The weapons of preference for killing animals and people were always an assegai, broad serrated-edge Zulu stabbing spear, and knobkerrie.

In contrast, this practice of remuneration was absolutely *verboten* in the Boer Transvaal Republiek, with a high probability of incarceration for the European trader, if caught.

Besides their two exploratory trips to Matabeleland and Mashonaland together from 1869 to 1872, Thomas Baines always stayed over en route at *Thorndale* farm in the Magaliesberg on his ox-wagon treks to Hartley Hills in the north or returning south again via Pretoria to Pietermaritzburg. Baines used that inland Natal Colony town as a logistics staging base for his explorations – within easy reach of Durban harbour.

Chapter 17:

Discoverer of ancient gold diggings in central present-day Zimbabwe in 1865

Rather than exploring the tsetse fly-infested Zambezi River Valley and visiting the Victoria Falls, the more entrepreneurial and ambitious Henry Hartley was much more interested in safely hunting for ivory and discovering the origins of payable gold mining reefs and other precious metal and gemstone deposits. He dared not admit this secret ambition to Mzilikazi or Lobengula. He would have been in clear violation of the exclusive verbal hunting licence granted to him.

On his wildlife hunting trip in 1865 an elephant he had shot for its ivory stumbled into a man-made depression, fell over and died. Henry Hartley immediately became intrigued by rose quartz reefs he found there and took samples for later assaying. Baines painted that epic scene at a later date from the descriptions that Henry provided. The painting is now in the Zimbabwe Archives and a copy is depicted below and on the cover page.

Painting by Thomas Baines from 1874 of a dying elephant falling into an old quartz pit of ancient gold diggings on his 1865 hunt

Henry invited German Explorer and prospector Herr Karl Mauch (1837–75) to accompany him on his next hunting trip in 1867, from March to December. Karl Mauch publicly announced his finding of gold in quartz reefs around Hartley Hills and Tati in a newspaper article published by the *Transvaal Argus* on December 1, 1867, and arranged for samples to be shipped back to London for assaying. Those samples were not all too exciting, but were enough to instigate Thomas Baines to establish the *South African Gold Fields Exploration Company* (SAGFE Co.) with his own and some London financers' limited equity capital for an "exploration company" and arrange to issue shares for a "working company". This was also the *raison d'être* for Baines accompanying Hartley on two exploratory expeditions to a place Baines named Hartley Town and Hartley Hills, in honour of Henry's "discovery of the Northern Gold Fields" near the Umvuli River.[1]

In 1869 Eduard Mohr, a wealthy German adventurer, amateur astrologist, hunter and gold seeker, accompanied Henry Hartley and Thomas Baines on their second expedition to further examine the central Matabeleland goldfields that Henry had uncovered on a hunting trip four years earlier.

Thomas Baines had unknowingly trekked with his ox-wagons on numerous occasions directly over and along the rich conglomerate outcrops of payable "Main Reef" gold and silver reefs of the Witwatersrand Gold Fields, around the future Johannesburg. He was not aware that the richest gold deposits in the world lay directly under the tracks of his ox-wagons trekking back and forth between Pietermaritzburg, Henry Hartley's *Thorndale* farm and Hartley Hills in Matabeleland/Mashonaland.

The gold quartz reefs at Hartley Hills were all but forgotten after that phenomenal discovery in 1886. And the future of the ZAR Transvaal Republic and South Africa changed forever.[2]

Even in 1874, six-months before he died, Thomas Baines was still trying to rescue his vision of a gold *Eldorado* at Hartley Hills, and still

---

[1] The town of Hartley is now renamed Ghegutu and the Umvuli River is now Munyati River in the central interior of Zimbabwe, near the capital city Harare (formerly Salisbury).

[2] It is ironic therefore that Thomas Baines spent so much time at Hartley Hills in Mashonaland between 1869 and 1872 prospecting for gold deposits. (Manuscript MS-049/10/1/1 of Thomas Baines's fieldnotes, Brenthurst Collection, 1871. Six samples dug up around August 6, 1869 and taken back to Pietermaritzburg and London for independent assaying by Messrs. Johnson, Matthey and Co. produced an average of 2.1 ounces of gold per ton for the selected sample – relatively disappointing. (Baines, Thomas, *Journal of 1877*, p. 30) Samples taken from the same area in 1872 showed better results of 3.1 ounces per ton of payable gold – Baines, Thomas, Papers. Original Field Notes of July 15, 1869 in a letter dated August 26, 1874. MS.049/6/5. The Brenthurst Library, Johannesburg

trying to pay off his substantial debts incurred on his second ox-wagon expedition, owed to Henry Hartley and others. (See the appendices for a facsimile of this graphite-pencilled, hand-written letter, transcribed below) . . .

Hartley Hill Gold Quartz Crushing Company Limited
Port Elizabeth 23rd October 1874

My Dear Mr. Hartley

I have great pleasure in informing you that the merchants of this town are organising a company under the above title for the purpose of working the reef you shewed me near Hartley Hill, Umvuli River. They have already subscribed liberally and I believe mean to carry the work on.

They are to buy the Machinery of the South African Gold Fields Company now in Durban and are to take my small battery also – giving me an interest in the company for it. I am not to receive any pay for three years but I am to have an interest in the success of the Company. I do not yet know how much but all these matters will be arranged soon, and I intend to devote the greater part of any profit that comes to me perhaps two-thirds or three-fourths to the payment of such debts as I incurred to such men as yourself, Mr. Lee or others in gaining the concession for the original Company.

With regard to that Company I am allowed to render it any friendly service that does not injure the interest of the Hartley Hill Company – and if it has discretion enough to avail itself of my friendship, I will put it in a way of paying itself yet.

I hope to start from Durban in March and I should be glad to know whether any of your sons or our friends the Jennings's are likely to be down and whether they would transport any portion of the Machinery to your farm Thorndale, or to Hartley Hill and at what rates.

The distance from Natal to your farm is 475 miles from Durban via Harrismith, Smut's Drift in the Vaal, and Potchefstroom, or via Heidelburg it is somewhat less.

The whole distance from Durban to Hartley Hill is 1212 miles.

I should like to know specially whether transport can easily be had at reasonable rates from your farm to Hartley Hill – for if this is difficult it will be better for me to buy all my own cattle and wagons in Natal – I should be glad if you would let me know the price of oxen in the Transvaal in good condition, free from sickness and ready to work.

I expect I shall have to ration from six to nine white men and I shall be glad to take as much of the provisions as possible from you.

Will you let me know the prices of Boers meal per muid, Salt pork, Bacon, Butter and dried fruit per 100 pounds. and goats or sheep each. There will be time to answer this letter – here as I shall certainly stay over November. and perhaps December too but I shall go to Durban as soon as the business of the Company is settled and I feel that my presence is required there.

I have a picture of "What led to the discovery of the Gold Fields". I sent you a newspaper with a notice of it. Watson recognised your likeness at once and even Mr. Robert White formally of Grahamstown who saw it in Natal recently asked without any prompting of any kind, was that not Hartley of Bathurst (?) – I will send you a photo but I think some little of the likeness is lost because the red of the face comes out darker than in the (original oil painting).

I am writing to Jewell – he is at Longpoort Mooi River Natal and has wagons, perhaps he may come up with me – I'm quite sure all your friends in Natal would wish me to send their kind regards of you to all friends and my kindest remembrances to yourself with sincerest sympathy for your late bereavement.

Believe me my dear Mr. Hartley

Your very sincere friend and fellow traveller

T. Baines

Side script on the handwritten letter: "I think I am going to send that picture to Dr Coverley who wishes me to paint twelve African elephants for a friend of his".

Dr Coverley was the Edinburgh-trained doctor at the Tati gold diggings (now Francistown, Botswana) who attended to Henry Hartley after his near fatal encounter with a white rhinoceros in November 1869. The picture that Baines is referring to is the one I have used to illustrate the discovery of ancient gold diggings at Hartley Hills on the cover page. (It is the epic oil painting that Baines completed in 1874 as part of a paid consignment of paintings done for German explorer Eduard Mohr, including the 1865 discovery). Hartley was in bereavement at the loss of his third wife, Mary Ann Maloney at the age of just 36, who had died at *Thorndale* on July 8, 1874. The Mr Jewell referred to in this letter is the wagon driver for Thomas Baines, as well as Secretary for the SAGF gold mining exploratory company and part-time photographer.

Earlier, on August 26, 1874 Thomas Baines sent a letter to the Secretary of the new "Quartz crushing company" setting out its structure and pro forma expenditures with £5,000 in capital, and £2,500 in working capital.

Copies of examples of those letters from the Brenthurst Collection of private papers are included as appendices to this book. Both Thomas Baines and Henry Hartley were dead by 1876 and nothing came of their gold mining business plans.

The SAGF Co. and its prospecting and mining concessions granted to Thomas Baines by Chief Lobengula were purchased by the British South Africa Chartered Company of Cecil John Rhodes for £5,000.[1]

---

[1] Bowen, J.A., *The Story of Hartley Hills* in the "Programme for the unveiling of the founding of the town on its 100th anniversary on 28th September 1969."

Inyateen July 4. 1869

T Baines Esqr

My Dear Sir

I fully Expected you before this but hope you will not be long behind us lighten your waggons all you can and follow as quick as you can minding to keep my trek Sir John is here but intends starting to morrow he has been trieing for a monopoly he is all self and most illiberal in all his dealings of any one that I have come in contact with he also has stated that your party are intirely under his direction and had he known of your approach he should have sent to stop your further progress of cours you know best and if he has that power why the gold fields will not be worked while he has or that the power is vested in him if I can possibly prevent it you know your authority and of cours know what to do this of cours is strictly Confidential,

best regards to all our friends

I remain

My Dear Sir

Yours Truly

H Hartley

Copy of anxious letter written on July 4th, 1869 by Henry Hartley and addressed to his travelling companion Thomas Baines from his hunting camp at Hartley Hills in central present day Zimbabwe (formerly Rhodesia) near the future City of Salisbury (now Harare)

Chapter 18:

Travelling companion & guide to British Explorer Thomas Baines

From April to December 1869, August to December 1870, and from May to June, 1871 Henry Hartley was a travelling companion and guide to Thomas Baines. Although Hartley said that he had known, by reputation, of the famous explorer Baines, they only met in person at *Thorndale* farm for the first time in April 1869.

Always the practical joker and feigning surprise, Hartley exclaimed to Baines: "I heard of your death some years before. How can I be persuaded that you are not a ghost?"[1] ... "But the justice I did to the good fare he set before us convinced him of his error!", Thomas responded. They got along well from that very first meeting.

Thomas and Henry became very good trusting, loyal friends to each other. Amazing individuals with unique insights, expectations and objectives. They clearly enjoyed discovering darkest Africa together. They were both blessed with high intelligence and ambition.

Henry Hartley had been on hunting and gold exploration trips to Matabeleland on at least three previous occasions, One in 1865 on his own when he discovered ancient tribal gold diggings, a second and third in 1866 and 1868 with Herr Karl Mauch to confirm the existence of payable gold deposits and to bring more ivory south.

The first exploratory expedition with Thomas Baines, led by Henry Hartley, set off from *Thorndale* farm in April 1869. It was on this trip that Hartley introduced Baines to the interim elderly Regent Um Nombata for the recently deceased King/Chief Mzilikazi, whom Hartley had met on numerous previous occasions.

There were also disagreements and personal conflicts with Sir John Swinburne and his competing and better financed *London and Limpopo Exploration Co.* party at Hartley Hills.

I am particularly intrigued by the ink-scripted letter of July 4, 1869 in Henry Hartley's own beautiful, Victorian-era, cursive hand-writing (MS 049/5. 48) addressed to Thomas Baines from where he was camped at Inyati, some distance south of Inyoka – "The Serpent" (later named Hartley Town and Hartley Hills). I wonder whether it was written with a hand-cut, porcupine quill pen using imported

[1] Baines, Thomas, *Journal of 1877*, p. 18

black ink from Europe, and whether the letter was hand-delivered promptly by a dispatch rider servant on horseback back along the rough ox-wagon track to Thomas Baines? Hartley was addressing his "strictly confidential" concerns on the bad behaviour, disloyalty and scheming "monopolistic and selfish" Sir John (Swinburne). He was asking Thomas Baines, who was following some distance behind Hartley and Sir John, to "follow as quickly as you can" taking their usual ox-wagon trekking route northwards. This letter from July 1869 alone tells us so much of Henry Hartley's character, insightful intelligence, gut-feelings, friendships and loyalties. He was very concerned to maintain his good and trusted relationship with Ndebele/Matabele Chief Mzilikazi (and his successor), and with Thomas Baines.

Baines decided to keep that important letter from his good friend, now preserved at the Brenthurst Library Collection of rare Africana in Parktown, Johannesburg.[1] It is one of the exceptionally rare letters remaining that Henry wrote himself. Hartley was asserting that Sir John Swinburne was ignoring all the verbal agreements he had made himself with Thomas Baines and the Matabele Royal Kraal.

As Simon Hartley (b. 1968), whose grandfather's grandfather is Henry Hartley, touchingly commented[2] . . . "There is something about a hand written note or letter that just wipes away the sands of time and puts you in the presence of the writer".

Sir John Swinburne, a British hereditary baronet, was attempting to usurp his perceived authority over Henry Hartley and Thomas Baines at the gold diggings at Hartley Hills. Hartley would have none of it, and complained to Baines in that letter.

Sir John lost his royal kraal mining concession when he failed to respect Matabele tribal traditions by not visiting the Royal Kraal on his way in or out of the sovereign Matabele territory and humbly offering his respects to the Paramount Chief. Sir John was forced to retreat with his quartz-crushing machinery to the Tati gold-bearing diggings in adjoining Bechuanaland. He soon became disillusioned with the results there and left for the newly-discovered diamond fields to try his luck in Kimberley.

On his first expedition trip north Thomas Baines was adequately funded by his London company. Not so on his final trip in 1871.

On Thomas Baines's final trip north in 1871, specifically to obtain confirmation in writing of his verbal agreement of April 9, 1869 with

---

[1] I was able to "marry" the content by examining the context in which it was written with Thomas Baines's 1877 book (pp. 25-29), his original diaries around July 1869, the large detailed black-and-white printed cadastral and geographic map that was produced by T. Baines FRGS in 1876, and T.V. Bulpin's 1965 interpretation (pp. 155-173) of the "same" incident.

[2] E-mail dated November 9, 2021.

Chief Lobengula, Henry did not accompany him all the way to the Royal Kraal at Bulawayo. London shareholders of the *Gold Fields of South Africa Exploration and Mining Company* were reluctant to advance any more cash to Baines until he provided written proof of that agreement. A vast, carefully defined territory of Matabeleland and Mashonaland were included in the written agreement, together with extensive and generous mining rights.[1]

Thomas Baines continued to make arrangements to formally float the successor company to the SAGFE & M. Co. in 1874, shortly before he died.

Thomas Baines died of dysentery on April 8, 1875 in Pietermaritzburg at the age of 55. Henry Hartley died a year later on February 8, 1876 at his *Thorndale* farm at the age of 60, probably from ongoing rib and internal injuries sustained from his "sad accident" on November 26, 1869,[2] from which he never fully recovered.

Sadly, Thomas Baines was no businessman, but he was meticulous and pedantic in writing down every "insignificant" geographic and cultural detail in his field notes, and kept a daily diary. He accurately sketched and painted thousands of scenes of his explorations and displayed them to members of the royal family in London. He published a book of sketches and paintings in London in 1864, especially oils of the Victoria Falls. Most of those original sketches are housed in the Natural History Museum in London. He was a Fellow of the Royal Geographic Society. He summarized his penciled field notes in a journal, which were published posthumously in 1877. He also compiled and published a detailed map of Southern Africa in 1876.[3]

Henry Hartley was much more low key and not much of a correspondent or record keeper. Most of the records that he did make, and correspondence that he did write, were burnt in a fire set at *Thorndale* homestead by the British Imperial Army during the Anglo-Boer War of 1899–1902. (More on that later). He was an astute businessman, an expert horseman and accurate marksman and concentrated rather on opportunities as they presented themselves, and on the tasks and issues at hand. But he and Thomas Baines made a good team with their divergent complimentary skills.

Thomas Baines had sailed from England to Durban in February 1869. He had heard about Henry's gold discoveries in Matabeleland – confirmed by prospector Karl Mauch.

---

[1] Baines, Thomas, *Journal of 1877*, p. 50
[2] Being trampled by a charging rhinoceros. Baines, Thomas, *Diaries of 1869–1872*, edited by Wallis, 1946, pp. 230 & 452
[3] His original field notes, correspondence and daily diaries are part of the Brenthurst Collection of priceless Africana, which I managed to access.

Sir John Swinburne, Bart. and some colleagues had "associated themselves under the title of the *London and Limpopo Mining Company*, with a steam traction engine" for crushing gold-bearing quartz ore[1] and trekked north. Simultaneously, a group of Thomas Baines's friends "enrolled themselves as the *South African Gold Fields' Exploration Company*" with Baines appointed to lead the prospecting expedition. Mr C.J. Nelson, a Swedish mineralogist, was appointed as the geologist and Mr R.J. Jewell was appointed as the Company Secretary.

On March 13, 1869 Baines and his party set out from his base in Pietermaritzburg across the Drakensberg to the British military border town of Harrismith on the Orange Free State grass highveld and then via Potchefstroom to *Thorndale* and the north. Each of his wagons was pulled by a span of six to eight oxen. They were loaded with bags of sugar, meal, dried fruit, biltong, flour, salt and all the necessary provisions for a long trek and exploration. They took along glass beads and reams of cotton cloth to trade with the local tribesmen. Baines and Hartley both carried a fully stocked pharmacy case filled with medicines, including ammonia, quinine and opium. They could shoot game for the pot along the way. Baines was well funded with British Sterling in cash on this first exploratory expedition. Pulling ox-wagons along the old rough hunter tracks was preferable in the dry winter months when the drifts across streams and rivers were low and shallow. It was much more difficult for the oxen to pull a wagon up a steep muddy incline or wade through a deep, swiftly-moving, muddy drift in the hot rainy season. The tsetse fly, tropical diseases and cattle flies were also less of a pest in the dry winter months between April and November.

Thomas preferred to travel on the ox-wagon, or walk alongside with his field book and pencil at the ready. He only kept horses for riding in emergencies. His headman, Inyassa, carried his heavy hunting rifle for him if he needed it. The local tribesmen they encountered along the way were rarely viewed as a threat to their safety.[2]

Henry Hartley always rode his favourite hunting horse, carrying his heavy, two-bore hunting rifle at the ready.

Besides taking sextant measurements for latitude, Baines also had a magnetic compass to determine direction, and used a tracheometer for measuring distance travelled – a distance-tracking, pedometer-type instrument that hung under the axle of an ox-wagon that was geared to the ox-wagon rear wheel spokes: He recorded 829 miles, 5 furlongs, 191 yards to the Tati gold fields[3] but the tracheometer was

[1] Baines, Thomas, *Journal of 1877*, p. 15
[2] Baines, Thomas, *Journal of 1877*, p. 27

not very accurate, particularly by Baine's rigorous expectations. A distance of 899 to 1,221 miles by ox-wagon one-way from Pietermaritzburg according to Thomas Baines's calculations depending on the route taken.

There was busy trade by ox-wagon between the sea port of Port Elizabeth, the Hartley family general store in nearby Bathurst with its wide range of Victorian goods, and the import of ivory and wild animal skins from the north through the newly-established Transvaal Republiek capital of Potchefstroom, back to Grahamstown. At the time most of the ivory that had not yet been hunted to virtual extinc-

[3] Reaching the Tati settlement on June 9th, 1869, Baines, Thomas, *Journal of 1877*, p. 7

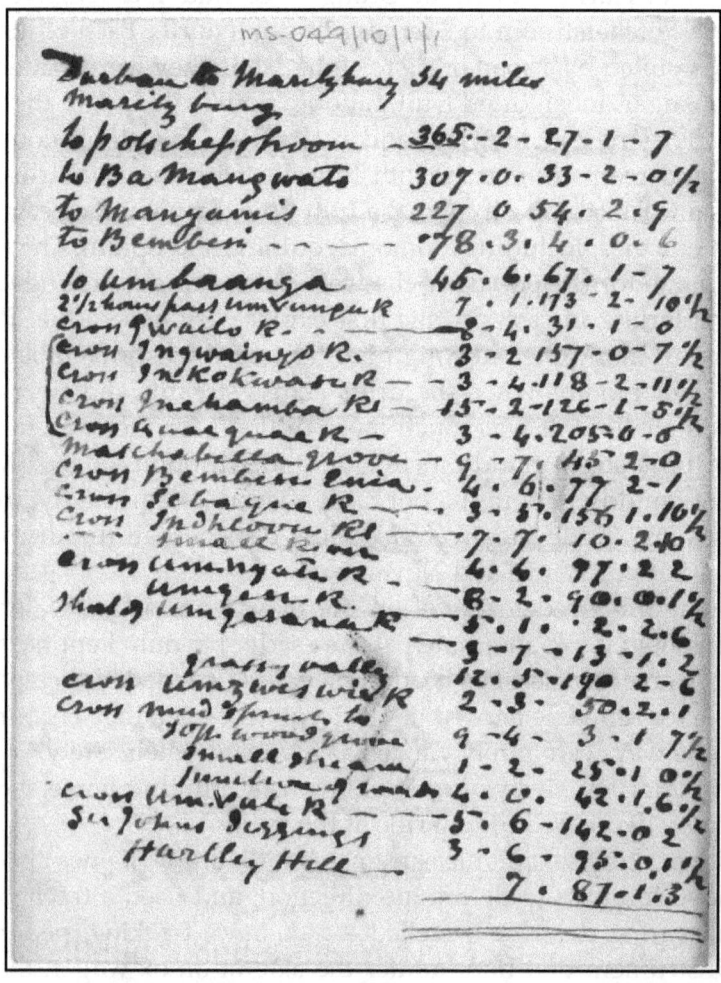

Tabulation by Thomas Baines of distance travelled in 1869 from Pietermaritzburg via Potchefstroom to Hartley Hills using a "tracheometer" *

* Baines, Thomas, Papers. Original Field Notes MS.049/10/1/1. The Brenthurst Library, Johannesburg

tion by white European settlers in the western and eastern Cape Colony was purchased by barter from native tribes to the north occupying Zululand, Bechuanaland, Matabeleland, Mashonaland and Barotseland. Native tribes drove their wild prey into narrow hidden screened carrells and then over a steep hidden ledge into large camouflaged pits that they dug where the animals were slaughtered with assegais and spears for barter and export to European ox-wagon traders like Henry Hartley.

Hartley almost certainly also kept extensive personal records of his explorations, but none exist today, having been destroyed during the hostilities of the Anglo-Boer War in 1899. I have been able to find only two letters written in Henry Hartley's own hand. One anxious letter written to his good friend, Thomas Baines; and another sad letter addressed to his eldest son Frederick. Facsimiles of those letters are included in the appendices and discussed in this book.

It is astonishing how efficient mail delivery was in those early days along the ox-wagon road north between traders and hunters. Letters and small parcels would be carried by runners or by horseback using domestic servants from one outspan camp to the next. The *Bush Telegraph* was fully operational. Even sophisticated banking and loan transactions, Bills of Exchange, IOUs, and other financial business were conducted along the route – besides barter, of course, with the local native inhabitants. They were illiterate and unfamiliar with coinage[1] and deferred banking. Many had never seen a horse or a rifle, and, until Henry Hartley arrived, had never seen a white man. Even cotton/linen cloth for making clothes was a novelty. Nevertheless, they had a highly sophisticated culture and governing hierarchy based on verbal agreements.

On his 1871 trip from Pietermaritzburg, Thomas Baines stopped at Rustenburg to collect English post delivered from Cape Town. Baines had recently been made Commander of the *South African Gold Fields Exploration Company's Expedition* by the main financial shareholders in London, but was most disappointed to learn en route that they were providing him with no further financial seed money for his second exploratory expedition. He also had to pay the Postmaster in Rustenburg 5 shillings in Excise Duty to receive his mail out of the sparse 10 shillings he still had in cash![2]

Almost every night Baines would take a sextant reading to determine his mean latitude in degrees, minutes and seconds by measur-

---

[1] Baines, Thomas, *Diaries of 1869–1872*, edited by Wallis, 1946, p. 65
[2] Baines, Thomas, *Diaries of 1869–1872*, edited by Wallis, Baines Goldfields Diaries, 1946, for diary entry of June 23, 1871, p. 621

ing the angle between the stars *Centauris* and *Arcturus* and the horizon at a predetermined time and adjust for an index error of two minutes. He could also check his accuracy by comparing the reading that he took at the same outspan on his previous trip north.

He was able to determine his line of longitude each day by waiting for the sun to reach its zenith at noon and cast its shortest shadow, and then measuring the time difference between Greenwich Mean Time and the time shown on his portable fob watch.[1]

Measuring longitude this way was less reliable than determining mean latitude with a sextant at night using a two minute interval for at least three readings.

For longitude your portable watch needed to be dead accurate in the bush. This was not the case in 1871. It had to be regularly checked for accuracy with professional astronomical observations of the relative positions of the four moons of Jupiter using a powerful telescope. And comparing them to a printed nautical table previously recorded at Greenwich outside London.

We know that Mohr was able to very accurately determine his latitude and longitude position in darkest Africa. He regularly measured solar, lunar and celestial distances and angles with his sextant and other geographic instruments. He was a proficient mathematician. When he finally arrived at Victoria Falls on June 20, 1870, which is also the southern hemisphere winter solstice, he was able to determine that his watch (chronometer) was running 12 minutes and 22 seconds fast; and thereafter able to determine his longitude with much greater accuracy.[2] Mohr and Baines would often compare their calculations at the same outspan resting spots and carve their geopositions in degrees, minutes and seconds into a tree trunk for the other to find and check. These etchings became "road signs" for other travellers to follow.

Secondly, trekking north of the Tropic of Capricorn meant that the shadow of the sun cast at noon was often almost directly overhead and therefore difficult to determine local noon time accurately.

In addition to plotting his longitude and latitude, Baines used "Dead Reckoning" with a magnetic compass. He measured distance travelled with a trocheometer. A multi-geared, Trocheometer box was fitted to the wheel of an ox-wagon calibrated to record measured miles, furlongs, yards, (feet and inches) travelled. Not very reliable

---

[1] There are 360 degrees of longitude around the globe, with each hour representing 15 degrees of longitude. 30 degrees of longitude translates to two hours on your watch. So, if your watch showed 14:01:01 at noon local time, it meant that your longitude was 30 degrees, one minute and one second east of GMT. The earth therefore rotates through one degree of longitude every four minutes.

[2] Mohr, p. 322

but could confirm geo-coordinate positions determined for longitude and latitude that were generally more accurate. If the wagon was going downhill fast on stony ground the wheel would often jump and under-read distance travelled.

Altitude was determined by the boiling point of water in degrees Fahrenheit with a mercury thermometer. The higher the elevation the lower the boiling point of water compared to mean sea level. A barometer, measuring air pressure, was also used to check the accuracy of elevation in feet above sea level independently, derived from the boiling point of water

When Baines wanted to transfer his longitude and latitude co-ordinates to create a map for himself and other fellow travelers he would set up an easel on the floor of his ox-wagon and chart a grid of lines on a sheet of paper, according to the desired scale. He would then plot his route coordinates with pin pricks through six sheets of paper. These pin pricks were then combined with observed cartographical physical features, such as rivers and place names onto an initial map.[1]

If he wanted to make copies of the map (or other important correspondence intended for more than one recipient) Baines would insert carbon paper between a maximum of three sheets of good white writing paper and press down hard with a constantly-sharpened graphite pencil. To keep the writing point sharp he used his penknife, so that the third bottom sheet was still legible. He would be able to hand those copies to the nearest "Post Office" runner for delivery to a fellow traveler who was following behind or one ahead of him along the ox-wagon road, or even back to Cape Town harbour for delivery by sailing ship to Great Britain.

On this second exploration, Baines caught up with Henry Hartley's ox-wagon train on June 23, 1871 near the Marico River crossing.[2]

Hartley was on his way north as far as the Tati gold diggings hunting elephants as usual, but also looking for outcrops of diamondiferous earth similar to that which had produced the Kimberle☐y Diamond Rush a few months earlier. The Kimberlite igneous pipes were producing enormous deposits of gemstones, that Cecil John Rhodes and a few of his business cohorts would soon monopolize.

If you were an alien observer in a capsule orbiting the earth in the 1860s, and looked down, you would observe a functioning, slow moving "caterpillar-like" train stretched along a rough 2,000 mile long gravel trading route from Port Elizabeth to Hartley Hills. Trek-

---

[1] This was not unlike what Captain James Cook so successfully accomplished in the 1770s on his exploratory sailings to the undiscovered Pacific Ocean when circumnavigating the world.

[2] Baines, Thomas, *Diaries of 1869–1872*, edited by Wallis, 1946, p. 622

king by ox-wagon with a heavy load of valuable ivory or imported Victorian goods was a frustratingly slow means of transport.

Baines was relatively clueless in understanding the "Matabele etiquette", and way of doing business, which Hartley had already fully internalized over the years – and respected for self-preservation as the first white man entering this dangerous Ndebele/Zulu Kingdom of aggressive warriors.[1]

Baines was keen for Henry Hartley to personally introduce him to the Matebele King, and negotiate on his behalf.

With the Ndebele/Zulu King Mzilikazi – Shaka's exiled nephew[2] – beginning to age in the late 1860s and "pushing his conquests as far as the Zambezi, he was informed of a conspiracy to dethrone him", and that his principal royal wife was about to appoint a successor heir upstart. This was not to King Mzilikazi's liking so he had all the inhabitants of the Kraal killed, except for a favoured child Lobengula,[3] by another lesser wife.

The Northern Ndebele/Zulu King of Matabeleland followed the Zulu practice of polygamous marriages. The more cattle you owned (which was a measure of your wealth) and the power you exerted, the more wives you could acquire through the lobola system.[4]

The Shona tribes in adjoining Mashonaland were terrified of King Mzilikazi and dared not hunt any of the king's wild animals, or prospect for metals or precious stones.

Mzilikazi died in September 1868 and an elder loyal regent took over the caretaker role until a new king was appointed.

On January 25, 1870 a Mr Lee, a missionary to the Matabele tribe, who was fluent in the local Northern Ndebele/Zulu dialect, received an invitation to attend the proclamation of the new successor Lobengula at the Royal Kraal at "Inthlathlangela" (present-day Inyati).[5]

9,000 to 10,000 warriors gathered in April 1870 for the ceremony, armed to the teeth with large ox-hide war-shields, short stabbing assegais, headdresses of black ostrich plume feathers, white cattle skins draping their arms and legs, and catskin kilts. They stamped

---

[1] Henry Hartley was fully aware of what had happened to Piet Retief and his party of Voortrekkers in Zululand when they tried to negotiate with the Zulu King Dingaan – the successor to "Napoleonic King" Shaka. The Voortrekker party were all murdered in his Royal Kraal at Eshowe in Zululand. This led to the Battle of Blood River on December 16, 1838

[2] Referred to as "Umselegazi" in Thomas Baines's *Journal of 1877*, p. 32

[3] Referred to as "Lo Bengula" in his *Journal of 1877*.

[4] The tradition of polygamous marriage carries on even today amongst traditional Zulus in Kwa-Zulu Natal. The now former Zulu-speaking third South African President Jacob Zuma has six wives, all housed at his extensive, tax-payer-funded homestead compound of Nkandla. He is currently facing "State Capture" corruption and Contempt of Court charges, and has been imprisoned (2022).

[5] Baines, Thomas, *Journal of 1877*, p. 33

their feet in unison, danced and shouted war chants. It must have been a frightening and memorable spectacle. About eight to ten white men mounted on horses also attended, including Willie Hartley, the 17 year-old son of Henry Hartley.[1] Dozens of cattle were slaughtered in a cruel manner for the feast that followed.

The newly-proclaimed King/Chief Lobengula (who ruled from April 1870 to 1893) seemed to be satisfied with Thomas Baines's credentials and announced to Mr Lee that Mr Baines "Can have the northern goldfields!" What did this actually mean? Baines was not sure. He went back to Lobengula's Royal Kraal to meet Lobengula in person.

> Other wagons stood near, laden with presents that had been made to his father, (Mzilikazi). Beads, guns, pistols, Colt's and other revolvers, corroded into masses of rust, and every conceivable article of use or luxury that a traveller could offer to a barbarian monarch, among which I will mention a splendidly mounted Scottish garter dirk and a pair of magnificent ram's horn mulls, mounted in massive silver.[2]

Mzilikazi was known as a ruthless leader, as was his chosen adopted son Lobengula, who succeeded him. Deneys Reitz in his *Triology of the Anglo-Boer War* written in 1929 (p. 413) repeats a story of a pioneer hunter friend that Lobengula

> ... kept tame crocodiles at a waterhole near his kraal. Offenders were bound hand and foot and placed beside the pool while the king sat watching the reptiles drag their victims under the surface. He also said that the first time Lobengula was presented with a rifle he amused himself by taking potshots at any of his subjects that happened to be passing and woe betide the unfortunate who attempted to evade the royal amenities by running too fast.

Whether this was true or not I do not know. Neither Thomas Baines nor Henry Hartley nor other pioneer hunters vouch for these happenings. Nor can crocodiles be tamed! The warriors were unfamiliar with European guns, and had difficulty in shooting straight.

It is known that crocodiles were regarded as superstitious villains in tribal mythology and that you should not eat the liver of a crocodile, lest you become possessed with witchcraft. Nor should any

---

[1] Henry Hartley was not present at the coronation as he had returned to *Thorndale* in December 1869 to recuperate after his almost fatal encounter with a white rhinoceros on November 26, 1869 near Mangwe.

[2] Baines, Thomas, *Journal of 1877*, p. 35

person have a dead crocodile in his possession. After shooting a crocodile to preserve its head, Baines was careful to dispose of the carcass.[1]

Baines particularly enjoyed the steaks cut from an eland over a barbeque and was not averse to eating the cooked flesh of a young crocodile, provided he avoided eating the liver! Henry Hartley made sausages from the meat of a giraffe and used the skin of a giraffe for making tough leather rope.

The President of Zimbabwe, Emmerson Mnangagwa (as of 2022) is colloquially known as "The Crocodile". Mnangagwa was a fierce lieutenant of his predecessor, despot President Robert Mugabe, in the Liberation War against Ian Smith and his ruling, minority white Rhodesian Front Party, prior to full independence in 1980. Mugabe died at the advanced old age of 95 in 2019.

Unless you attended a missionary school and were taught reading, writing and arithmetic by European teachers you remained illiterate in writing. You certainly did not understand the nuances of legal documents written in the English language. Thus the reliance on verbal agreements. The Matabele relied on a deep verbal belief culture where verbal agreements and respect for the chief were paramount. Henry Hartley understood this "Matabele etiquette". Thomas Baines and other European explorers did not.

However, respect for one's personal possessions was not part of the bantu culture, unless you were a revered chieftain. Petty theft was. Stealing cattle from each other's clans was a national pastime.

Many had not seen a horse, a gun or a white man, had no knowledge of writing, reading or arithmetic, and no knowledge of coinage (except glass beads and animal hides and ivory). They bartered goods for economic exchange. They had never seen a paved road or mountain tunnel or a railway line. But they certainly understood tribal customs like *lobola*, and absolute loyalty to the king or paramount chief.

While a verbal agreement was perfectly acceptable to Chief Mzilikazi and Lobengula, – even insisted upon – it was not to the satisfaction of the SAGF Exploration and Mining Company shareholders back in the City of London. Baines had to return to the Royal Kraal in 1871 to confirm that verbal agreement in writing, sealed and witnessed by both parties. By then it was too late. The shareholders were no longer keen on pursuing the extensive mining rights that Baines and Hartley had negotiated.[2]

---

[1] Ibid, p. 41
[2] April 6, 1869 marked the date of "completion" of the verbal agreement. Baines, Thomas, *Journal of 1877*, p. 36

I was also particularly interested in Thomas Baines's original field notes of July 15th, 1869[1] preserved in The Brenthurst Library, Johannesburg. Baines seems to be drafting random notes to himself for discussion and negotiation with others. They are not repeated in either his published personal diary, nor his published journal, for that same day! But, significantly they do express in writing what he was actually thinking at the time for us to review, nearly two hundred years later . . .

> . . . The Chief of the Matabele to be offered 1,000 cows for the right of mining of the Northern Goldfields and the Exclusive Privilege of working them. The Company to have the Exclusive Rights of mining within such limits as may be agreed on . . .
>
> . . . 300 shares or more, at the discretion of the Company, to be granted to Mr. Hartley in consideration of his services in assisting the Expedition to reach the Gold Fields, and 100 or more to Mr. Malony (Henry Hartley's stepson) in consideration of his Assistance . . .
>
> . . . All offences committed by white men to be tried by white men in the presence of a native Chief, and all offences by natives against whites to be tried by Native Chiefs in the presence of a white man[2] . . .
>
> . . . Proposals of amalgamation on equal terms to be made to the London & Limpopo Company, and all other gold seekers working in lands granted to the Company to pay to the company a tariff of ? or whatever tariff the Government may impose.[3]

On October 3, 1869 the "Matabele army returned with plunder from a successful foray against the Mashona warriors all day long", Baines wrote in his field notes, but did not repeat them in either his diaries or his journal of the same date![4]

After several meetings with the newly-coronated King/Chief Lobengula in April 1870 defining the geographic boundaries of his prospecting concession, he granted Thomas Baines permission to "go

---

[1] Baines, Thomas, Papers. Original Field Notes of July 15, 1869. MS.049/9.2 (pp. 104-6)
[2] It is noteworthy that in these pre-colonial encounters between white Europeans representing a technically-advanced Enlightenment Era culture; and native warriors, there was already a spirit of cooperation and conciliation between the very different cultures, rather than domination. The Matabele tribe were deemed by most white explorers at the time to be mere savages.
[3] *The London & Limpopo Exploration Company* was led by their archrival Sir John Swinburne, who was prospecting in the same area as Thomas Baines and Henry Hartley in 1869, and was better financed and equipped with steam-driven, quartz-crushing equipment to extract gold from the raw ore.
[4] Baines, Thomas, Papers. Original Field Notes of October 3, 1869. MS.049/9.3 (p. 74). The Brenthurst Library, Johannesburg

in and seek and dig for gold anywhere within those limits".[1] In exchange Baines gave Lobengula a salted horse,[2] saddle, bridle and rifle to the value of £100.

The new paramount chief objected to Baines flying the white-bordered Union Jack on his wagons, because it "drove away the rain" in their tribal mythology, but "there was no harm in the red ensign of the (Natal Colony) flag so long as it hung quietly, and did not flutter in the wind".[3]

In hindsight, Lobengula must have been very pleased with the negotiations. Baines negotiated one thousand head of cattle, gifted to the king and a nicely polished old hunting rifle, and horse & saddle, in exchange for a mining permit to dig and extract gold within his territory. All that Baines was able to show the Chief on exiting his kingdom at the end of his first prospecting exploration in December 1869 was a bag of gold-bearing white quartz rock with almost no visible gold in it. A really good deal from Lobengula's perspective! The Thomas Baines party spent Christmas 1869 at the Tati River gold diggings in Bechuanaland.

Baines was pleased, but surprised, to record the comment by the Matabele Royal Kraal hierarchy that, "Yes, we are glad the King has given Baines the goldfields". Verbal agreements were sacrosanct in the absence of reading or writing in their culture. They did not understand the concept of individual freehold land ownership. What was meant was that a hunting and prospecting licence had been granted for an undefined limited period. But, invasion, possession, and subjugation by a victor of the victim were concepts that they had fully internalized.

Once the party had returned to Hartley Hills, after attending the coronation of Lobengula in April 1870, Baines had a simple two-roomed, wattle-and-daub-walled, thatch-roofed hut built for himself for the duration of his stay while prospecting the area. He used hard-wooded, Mopani poles for the structure. Mopani also produced a resinous gum, which the white ants would not touch.[4]

On July 5, 1870 Tom Maloney (Henry Hartley's stepson) and a hunting colleague, Leask, arrived back at the highveld Hartley Hills outpost with the devasting news that all members of the party of hunters that had proceeded down to lower elevations to hunt for elephants had suffered from malaria, tsetse fly, and other sub-tropical

---

[1] Baines, Thomas, *Journal of 1877*, p. 37
[2] A "salted" horse that had deliberately been infected with distemper, recovered, and was thereafter immune from this deadly disease.
[3] Baines, Thomas, *Journal of 1877*, pp. 38 & 43
[4] Completed on April 25, 1870, Baines, Thomas, *Journal of 1877*, p. 39

diseases.[1] Seven members of the hunting party had died. This included Henry Hartley's biological son, Willie. Willie had died of blackwater fever and was immediately buried in a shallow grave on May 29, 1970 at the young age of seventeen.[2]

Henry Hartley, who was hunting in a separate area to the east, arrived back at Thomas Baines's outspan camp on August 20, 1870 to learn of the news for the very first time, and was "overwhelmed with grief for the loss of his favourite son".[3]

They all immediately proceeded on horseback to visit the grave some 22 miles distance away. But, as usual, Henry Hartley followed his instinct, rather than his heightened emotions. Along the way he spotted elephant spoor within half-a-mile of the grave site. Following elephant spoor immediately became a first priority. Resting at his son's grave to mourn could wait, notwithstanding his personal grief. The elephants would not wait, and his much-loved son would not move position!

---

[1] Baines, Thomas, *Diaries of 1869–1872*, edited by Wallis, 1946, p. 454; and Leask, Thomas, *Southern African Diaries of 1865–1870*, edited by Wallis, 1954, p. 212

[2] W.J.H., 29/5/70" was marked on a tree at the gravesite, Baines, Thomas, *Journal of 1877*, p. 41

[3] ibid, p.41. Also Baines, Thomas, *Diaries of 1869–1872*, edited by Wallis, 1946, p. 448

Extract of sketch by Thomas Baines of his "house" under construction at Hartley Hills ancient gold diggings with Henry Hartley digging for gold-bearing quartz in the foreground (photo taken courtesy of Michael Tucker at the Archives of Zimbabwe)

Does this display a hard heart and little respect for his son who was dead, and a greater urgency to make more money from valuable ivory?

Or, does this explain the calm, focused nature that Henry Hartley was capable of expressing in such dire circumstances, and his typical behavioural trait of subjugating his emotions to the actual important task at hand.

Who knows?

"Mr. Hartley shot two, and the other three hunters one each" – a lucrative hunt.

Both Henry Hartley and Thomas Baines were most anxious not to transgress the separate permissions granted by Lobengula. Hartley could hunt for ivory, but not prospect for minerals. Baines could prospect for gold and dig trenches, but not hunt. They were fully aware that there were spies and Matabele minders following their exploits closely and would report back any transgressions of their verbal agreements to their King Lobengula, on their return to the Royal Kraal at Bulawayo.

The subservient Mashona tribe, who were predominant around Hartley Hills, were also most reluctant to even suggest any transgression of hunting animals or extracting gold ore in the dominant Matabele tribal territory. They were understandably terrified of the consequences.

It is ironic that following the Liberation war against Ian Smith for full independence in 1980, the roles were reversed. The Mashona tribe, under the newly-elected Prime Minister Robert Mugabe, became dominant and defeated the followers of Matabele leader Joshua Nkomo in a terrible genocidal massacre carried out by imported North Korean mercenary soldiers in the mid-1980s. Mashona domination persists today.

On their return southwards on November 23, 1870,[1] Henry and Thomas had an obligatory dinner with Lobengula at the Royal Kraal to pay their respects to the Ndebele king on exiting the king's territory. They also verbally reaffirmed their hunting and mining licences. They learnt that two divisions of the Matabele army had just returned from a raid on the Mashona, having killed 200 men, women and children and taken 8,000 head of cattle.

On that occasion, warriors returning from the battle demonstrated their own ferocity to the chief by cruelly killing a "stout and fierce young bull" and began eating it on the spot while still alive. In its death throes the infuriated bull fatally gored one of Thomas Baines's

---

[1] Baines, Thomas, *Journal of 1877*, p. 44

Thomas Baines sketch of the gravesite with the inscription: Willie Hartley's grave about 12 miles south east (magnetic) of Hartley Hill. T. Baines, August 29, 1870

Sketch of grave site of Willie Hartley drawn by Thomas Baines (W.J.H. 29/5/70) and photograph taken by R.J. Jewell (courtesy of Michael Tucker for the History Society of Zimbabwe)

This photograph of Willie's grave was taken in August 1870, by Robert Jewell, who accompanied Henry Hartley and Thomas Baines and Thomas Leask to the site and is almost identical to Baines sketch above.

special "salted" riding horses, which was "almost impossible to replace".[1]

Thomas Baines reached Pietermaritzburg on January 30, 1871 after staying over again with Henry and his wife at *Thorndale*. In his posthumously published journal of 1877 Baines again expressed his gratitude to Henry, "and was again indebted to him for many acts of kindness which were of the greatest possible service to me".

Baines left for the north again on May 16, 1871 on his second and final exploratory expedition.

On his way on horseback from his base in Pietermaritzburg to join Henry Hartley on his trek northwards, Baines stopped off nightly at random Voortrekker homesteads along the route to seek overnight accommodation.

The often very poor Afrikaner farmers were always most hospitable in their generosity, graciously sharing their limited food and small farm cottages with total white strangers. Warm water and a dry towel was handed out, a hot evening meal was shared with the unexpected

---

[1] Baines, Thomas, *Journal of 1877*, pp. 45 & 47. Baines, Thomas, *Diaries of 1869–1872*, edited by Wallis, 1946, p. 553

Sketch of Thomas Baines and King Lobengula – dressed in European attire – at post-battle celebrations following a cattle raid on the Mashona (courtesy of Michael Tucker)

travelling guest, as well as coffee and breakfast in the morning. A sheep skin blanket and an ample feather bed was laid on a space on the floor. When it came to pay for the overnight accommodation and meals the next morning the answer was inevitably: "No, it was a pleasure to have you visit us, and bring us news from the outside world". These simple white Afrikaner farmers would only accept nominal payment for his horse's fodder. The *vrou* of the house would also often deep-fry *vetkoek* (bread) in lard for the guest to carry as *padkos* together with some hard biscuits.

Baines caught up to Henry Hartley's party on June 23, 1871, already en route northwards, outspanned just beyond the Elands River crossing, north of Rustenburg. The moon was setting and becoming quite dark to continue riding on horseback. Baines writes: "Everyone was asleep, except the pack of fierce watch dogs, but some of them recognized me and became quiet. I waked one of the boys and asked him to give me a skin or a blanket of some sort without waking his master. But Mr. Hartley soon looked out and, expressing his surprise and pleasure at seeing me, dressed himself and came out, put a couple of large home-made sausages (giraffe venison) on the fire for me, after which we had a long conversation respecting our doings since we last parted and our plans for the future."[1]

Henry Hartley was very ambitious in acquainting his sons at a young age to hunting big game and exploring the subcontinent by ox-wagon and horse.

His fourth son "Harry" accompanied his father and mother with Thomas Baines's party on their trip to Tati in eastern Bechuanaland in June and July of 1871. **Harry was only ten years old at the time.** His mother Mary Ann Maloney, a widow – and Henry's third wife – also went along in the ox-wagon.

"Harry", Henry Albert Rorke Hartley, born on *Thorndale* farm on November 21, 1860 must have been a brave little pre-teen with a lot of *chutzpah*,[2] as well as total trust in his father on such a perilous journey. On the afternoon of July 17, 1871, one of Henry's hunting assistants shot a giraffe some distance from their outspan, which Thomas Baines wanted to sketch and measure for his fauna records. Baines borrowed Henry Hartley's horse and the ten-year old Harry had no hesitation in mounting his own little mare and accompanying Baines. They searched for the carcass until sunset without success, even with the hunting party shouting and firing identifying gunshots into the air. Baines made a warm fire by "breaking up cartridges and

---

[1] Baines, Thomas, *Diaries of 1869–1872*, edited by Wallis, 1946, pp. 622 & 645
[2] "conspicuous or flagrant boldness".

firing the loose powder, with a piece of rag". They used bushes to make a scherm to protect them and their horses from the jaws of any prowling leopard, hyena or lion.

Harry's mother was certainly relieved to see her little boy again the following day when they returned to camp. "Mr. Hartley complimented me by saying that he had no anxiety for his son so long as he was with me", Baines was pleased to record in his diary of Tuesday, July 18, 1871.[1]

While Hartley's party turned around after reaching the Tati River gold diggings settlement, Baines carried on northwards to Lobengula's Royal Kraal near Bulawayo.

Also in the company of his eldest son, Frederick Hartley, the ever ambitious father was intent on finding another *Eldorado* – this time exploring for similar diamondiferous earth found at the recently discovered Kimberley diamond diggings. That volcanic diamondiferous pipe had already produced huge quantities of highly valuable diamond gemstones and attracted tens of thousands of diamond seekers from all over the world, including Cecil John Rhodes.

This time Baines obtained a formal written agreement written in simple non-legal English, to mine for gold in the whole of Matabeleland. It was translated verbally into the local Zulu dialect, explained in detail to the King by Mr Lee – the missionary/hunter at nearby Mangwe – and signed by Lobengula on August 29, 1871 (reiterating his previous verbal agreement of April 9, 1870). The written agreement was witnessed by three representatives from each party. Lobengula signed with an "X" and affixed his personal seal of consent in wax with his boxwood carved emblem.[2]

On his second trek north to obtain the full agreement, Thomas decided to take a more direct return route back south, independent of Henry, but which necessitated travelling through tsetse fly invested bushveld direct to Pretoria.

His return trip from September to December of 1871 from Bulawayo[3] took Thomas Baines on a theoretically shorter, more direct southern route across the Limpopo, then along the Nylstroom River, through the Afrikaner Boer hamlet of Potgietersrus, and up along the Apies River to Pretoria.

It was not a good choice. He barely survived through lack of drinking water for his trekking team and oxen, as well as having to circumnavigate the tsetse fly areas in the heat of summer. Tsetse fly, malaria, black-water fever, yellow fever and other sub-tropical diseases were

[1] Baines, Thomas, *Diaries of 1869–1872*, edited by Wallis, 1946, p. 646
[2] Baines, Thomas, *Journal of 1877*, p. 50
[3] Baines, Thomas, *Diaries of 1869–1872*, edited by Wallis, 1946, p. 744

very prevalent within the lowland ravine valleys of the Zambezi and Limpopo Rivers.[1] Also the local black tribes were very wary of the Matabele warriors north of them and the white "Dutch-speaking" Voortrekker Afrikaners in the south. Both were aggressive enemies. They were, however, prepared to help the English-speaking traders and hunters in finding safe routes, provided that they would supply them with European hunting rifles, blocks of lead for making bullets, and gunpowder. It was a very serious offence within the Transvaal Rebubliek to provide European rifles to the local tribesmen.

Henry Hartley was much wiser to take the longer route back to his farm at *Thorndale* near Rustenburg, following the more open traditional Old Hunters' ox-wagon road that he had pioneered himself through the more open savannah bush along the edge of the Kalahari Desert within the British Protectorate of Bechuanaland. Tsetse fly were not as prevalent, and the road was well travelled, having been established by herds of elephants eons earlier for their migratory routes. The elephant pathways were replaced by pioneer ox-wagon tracks, then railway lines and finally by motor vehicle roads.

The only remedy that Thomas Baines could adopt on his last southern return from Bulawayo was to keep a vigilant lookout for the presence of any tsetse fly and immediately treat the puncture wound on an animal or human being with neutralizing ammonia. They had to carefully follow the spoor tracks of hunters' ox-wagons in the far north-western Transvaal and consult the local tribes to determine where pockets of tsetse fly would be found and therefore avoid trekking through those areas. These were often characterized by low-lying, ravine valleys and dense wooded areas. Drinking water for man and beast was also in critically short supply. One could avoid the worst of the fly by trekking by moonlight through known tsetse fly areas, when the deadly insects were not active, and outspanning during the daylight hours in an open savannah area. Losing a horse or an ox to the insect could place the whole journey in serious jeopardy.[2]

---

[1] Hartley's son, Willie, had died of fever the previous year while hunting in such areas.

[2] If you have been bitten by a tsetse fly, as I have (while on a game viewing trip into the Okavango Swamps in central Botswana in the 1970s) you know all about it with its sharp painful bite that often develops into fever within a few days, and then sleeping sickness. Your head feels like bursting with crushed glass inside, but fortunately getting a neutralizing injection from a doctor almost immediately relieves the fever and the pain. This was not so in 1871, when domestic animals and human beings would often die from being bitten by a single tsetse fly within days. On the other hand, wild animals are not affected at all, as they enjoy the benefits of life-long immunity. Even David Livingstone followed a higher elevation route away from, but parallel to the Zambezi River when he completed his transcontinental walk across southern Africa from Luanda on the Atlantic Ocean to Senna at

On November 24, 1871 after completion of his second and final expedition he and Mr R.J. Jewell, his wagon driver and photographer, rode the 47 miles from Pretoria along the Magaliesberg Valley to *Thorndale* to again visit with Henry Hartley and his family.[1]

As mentioned, when Thomas Baines arrived at the post office in Rustenburg on June 23, 1871 he had only 10 shillings left in his pocket for his second trip to Bulawayo to meet with Chief Lobengula yet again, and had to pay 5 shillings in excise duty to receive international correspondence. He received a letter in Rustenburg via Cape Town from Mr Oliver, the Secretary for the South African Gold Mining (SAGF) company in London, with the disheartening news that no further exploratory funds would be advanced for his second expedition trip. The only trading goods that Baines had was his ox-wagon, a horse, his hunting rifle, very limited dry provisions; plus glass beads and reams of cotton cloth to barter for provisions en route.[2]

Henry Hartley was kind enough to switch out horses and oxen for better healthier ones to enable Thomas Baines to reach the Royal Kraal north of Tati. Hartley was only intent on travelling as far as the Tati gold digging settlement before returning to his farm.

For Thomas Baines to restock his stores at Hartley Hills in December 1869, he had bought a substantial quantity of dry provisions and barter goods and goats and sheep from a Mr Behrens, an ox-wagon trader from Durban, with IOUs drawn on the SAGF company.[3]

Baines had also purchased a substantial amount of dry provisions that he needed at a very reasonable price of £40 from Mr Hartley, on August 21, 1870. Hartley was asked to submit his bill for payment to Mr Oliver in London, which he did, together with other more substantial debts owed by Baines as the leader of the SAGF Exploration Company. Hartley had just arrived at Hartley Hills from *Thorndale* on a hunting and trading trip.

In the absence of any ready hard £ sterling currency, Hartley and all the other debtors had to accept promissory notes from Baines in payment, to be drawn on the SAGF Exploration company at a later date.[4]

The only way that Baines could generate any real income was from painting commissions. Eduard Mohr, the wealthy German adventurer and fellow explorer paid Baines £100 for a few paintings.[5] These

---

the mouth of that mighty river on the Indian Ocean in 1855.

[1] Baines, Thomas, *Diaries of 1869–1872*, edited by Wallis, 1946, p. 700, and pp. 108 & 110 of MS.049/10/2

[2] Baines's Diary for June 23, 1871, p. 621

[3] December 14, 1869, p. 285

[4] August 21, 1870 p. 451. 180lbs of flour, 100lbs of coffee, 100lbs of sugar, bars of steel, a mining shovel & pick, etc.

included the iconic oil paintings of Victoria Falls when Baines visited there in 1862, and market square in Pietermaritzburg at the start of their expeditions to Matabeleland in March 1869 (now housed in the Zimbabwe Archives).

Frederick Hartley, Henry's eldest son, provided Baines's wagon driver Mr Jewell with a team of oxen from *Thorndale* for the second journey to the north. Hartley was away at the time.[1] Tom Maloney,

[5] December 13, 1869, p. 235 – £100 Sterling in 1869 is equivalent to ± £12,700 today.
[1] June 20, 1871, p.619

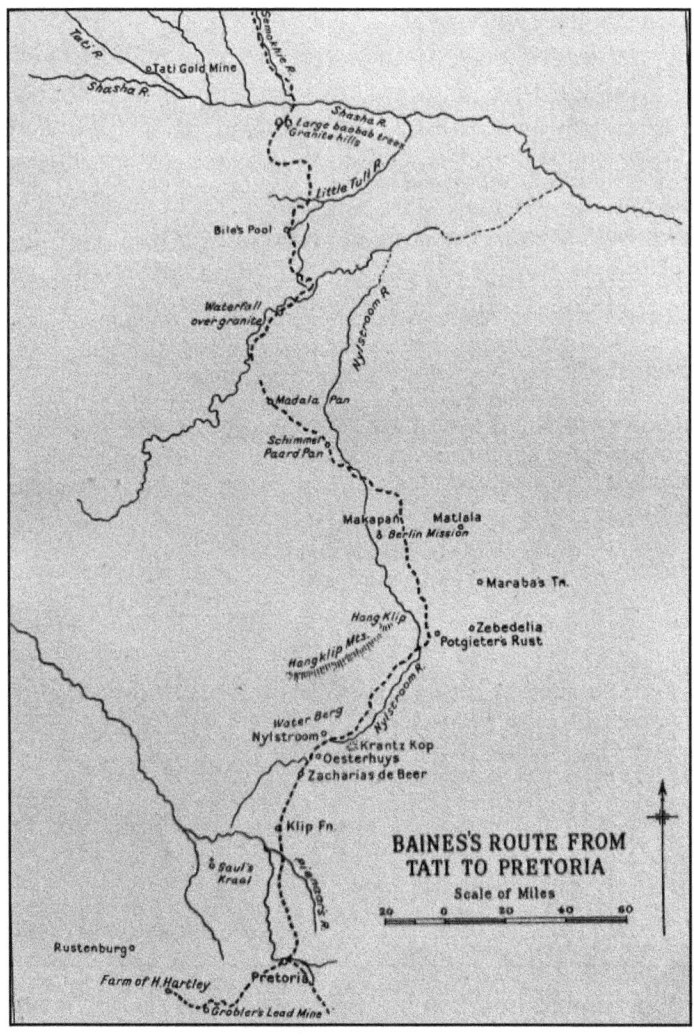

Return route map that Thomas Baines took from Bulawayo to *Thorndale* farm in the Magaliesberg arriving on November 24, 1871

his step-son, had sold a horse to Baines for £30 "to be paid by a bill on my pay", at a later date.[1]

On completion of his second expedition[2] Baines and Jewell arrived back in Pretoria from the north. He picked up a letter at the post office there from Henry Hartley "informing me that the bills I gave him in payment for horses and provisions had been returned from England, dishonoured, and that in consequence he (Hartley) would withdraw his application for shares and have nothing to do with the company at all, unless good security were given him; but as a friend he would be glad to do any personal service for me or Mr. Jewell". Baines also received a letter from Mr Oliver in Pretoria, portending the end of the SAGF Exploration company.

Thomas Baines, together with Jewell, then travelled to visit Henry Hartley to the west on his Magaliesberg farm and reached there on Saturday, November 25, 1871. They "parked" their two wagons and oxen there while Baines investigated other nearby gold diggings on horseback.

Baines travelled from Pretoria again on New Year's Day 1872 to try to "mend fences" with his good friend, "who still received me (and Mr. Jewell) kindly, though he feels very much hurt at the manner in

[1] July 12, 1870, p. 396
[2] November 23, 1871, p. 754

Thomas Baines painting of the wagons lined up at Pietermaritzburg for Matabeleland - Courtesy on Zimbabwe National archives

Painting commissioned by German adventurer Eduard Mohr of his and Thomas Baines's ox-wagon trains leaving Pietermaritzburg Market Square in March 1869 – each flying their respective North German and Union Jack national flags.

which the Company have treated him . . . (and) has no further confidence in the Company". Henry Hartley was furious. He had virtually financed Baines's entire second expedition, incurring considerable personal expenditure. As a result "he detains one waggon as a partial security for the bills due to him and I leave my horse Pleit in his care. I find that 9 oxen (left as security at *Thorndale* after his return) have died from tsetse". Baines also had to return two oxen to Hartley's neighbour, Mr G. Jennings, "as I am unable to pay him for the two I bought of him; and this leaves me a very weak span indeed for the remaining waggon"[1] for his return trek to his base at Pietermaritzburg, 450 miles away. One has to feel for Thomas Baines.

This was notwithstanding that by this time Baines had successfully negotiated a formal written concession from Chief Lobengula as per the April 9th, 1869 verbal agreement. But, it was too late.

It took from five to eight months for a letter to get to London and back to Hartley Hills along the rough ox-wagon tracks and slow sailing ship from Cape Town, so the company shareholders in London were unaware of the success that Baines had, in the interim, actually achieved in obtaining written, signed, witnessed and sealed confirmation of his comprehensive exploration and mining concession for almost the whole of the sovereign kingdom of Matabeleland and its adjoining vassal territory of Mashonaland. A phenomenal achievement.

The shareholders in London had already lost interest in spending any more capital funding for the SAGF Exploration Company. What the northern goldfields were actually worth had to wait until 1893 when Cecil John Rhodes invaded and colonized Matabeleland, killing Chief Lobengula and thousands of his tribesmen, and renaming the country after himself.

Hartley died on his Magaliesberg farm in 1876.

---

[1] January 1, 1872, p. 771

Chapter 19:

... And what became of his four hunting sons and stepson?

Henry Hartley's four biological sons Frederick, Thomas John, Willie and "Harry" all played prominent roles in his professional elephant hunting, gold and diamond exploration, and trading adventures. His stepson, Tom Maloney from his third marriage, whom he adopted, was also an integral part of the family businesses. Henry Hartley, as the patriarch, was an ambitious driving example for an integrated, focused family.

But, the Henry Hartley family were conflicted politically. At various times they supported the aggressive exiled Zulu Chief Mzilikazi and his successor Chief Lobengula in Matabeleland against the more placid Mashona and other indigenous resident tribes. His sons fought on both sides of the two Anglo-Boer Wars after "Ouda Baas" died, sometimes supporting the British Imperialists and 1820 English Settler colonists, and at other times supporting the semi-independent Afrikaner Boers in the ZAR Transvaal Republiek. His stepdaughter Emily Sarah Maloney of Irish heritage, from his third marriage, married his biological second son Thomas John, from his first marriage. This added to the conflicted political loyalties.

First son, Frederick, tobacco and coffee farmer (1844–1902)

Besides hunting for ivory with his father in the 1860s and 1870s and searching for payable diamondiferous pipes, Frederick was instrumental in developing the agricultural potential of their Magaliesberg farms.

When he came of age, Frederick moved to an adjoining farm, named Vaalbank No. 98 – also on the Magalies River – immediately to the south of *Thorndale*. He started a tobacco factory there named F.H. Hartley & Sons. They manufactured Hartley's cigarettes and Hartley's pipe tobacco, and operated a water-powered grain mill. The tobacco was also used in nicotine dips for cattle.[1]

Sarah Hartley (b. 1847 née Jennings from nearby Nooitgedacht farm) and wife of Frederick Hartley had the St Thomas Anglican Church built on *Thorndale* farm in 1884. They had five children.

[1] Berrington, Aileen, 1987, p. 196

The Jennings family must have been devout Anglicans. Bishop Bousfield, the Anglican Bishop of the Diocese of Pretoria, especially rode on his horse from Pretoria to consecrate the new St Thomas Church in 1885. (The mining camp of Johannesburg did not even exist at that time). The Reverend Richardson, the priest for Rustenburg, used to ride out to Nooitgedacht farm on horseback to hold communion in the Jennings's homestead Drawing Room on Sundays.[1] The Jennings family then built St Anne's Anglican Church at Hekpoort. That church is still fully functional. Several of the Jennings family are buried alongside the attractive little yellow-brick St Anne's Church.

The Jennings family were also 1820 Settlers, close friends of the Hartley family, whose father and sons regularly went elephant hunting in Matabeleland as part of Henry Hartley's hunting parties.

Second son, Thomas John, fighting with the Boers, 1899 (1846–1899)

Like his older brother, Thomas John Hartley was also given an adjoining farm by his father called Witfontein No. 102, to the west.[2] He also inherited the prime, remaining central portion of his father's farm, *Thorndale* No. 100, together with the original homestead. Ownership would have typically passed on to the eldest brother, Frederick.[3]

Thomas John had to have his arm amputated as a young man while setting a trap for a leopard, and the gun went off accidentally.

Family loyalties were very divided between supporting the Boer commandos who roamed the Transvaal farms to commandeer young men to fight against the British. There was no free choice. While his sons, who happened to be visiting relatives in the British-ruled Cape Colony, stayed and volunteered for the British forces there, Thomas joined the Boer forces in the Transvaal during the second Anglo-Boer War in 1899, together with his nephews and Harry, his younger half-brother. Thomas John was shot and killed right at the start of the war during the Siege of Ladysmith. The nephews – Frederick's two sons – then returned home and switched sides by joining the British forces, while Harry carried on supporting the Boer side until the end of the war in 1902.

There is not much available written by Henry Hartley himself, because the British Imperial soldiers burnt down the family homestead with its precious archives on his family farm at *Thorndale* in the Magaliesberg in 1899, when they learned that Henry Hartley's sec-

---

[1] Sanders, Muriel H., "Glimpses of the Past", 1973, on Jennings family history, p. 39
[2] Berrington, Aileen, 1987, p. 208
[3] Perhaps Henry Hartley was still holding a residual grudge against Frederick after their estrangement in 1870, and disinherited him, but that is pure speculation.

ond-born son had been "disloyal" by joining with the Boers at the start of the Anglo-Boer War. Thomas John Hartley (b. 1846 Somerset East – d. 1899 Pieters Hill skirmish) was killed near Colenso in the Natal Colony frighting for the Transvaal ZAR under Kommandant Louis Botha.

The British Imperialists already knew where *Thorndale* farm was located, merely by examining their 1899 Map of Southern Africa published by Stanford and Company in that year and shown in the Appendices. They took retribution by first confiscating, occupying and then burning down the Hartley homestead and all its priceless artifacts – including iconic paintings by Thomas Baines. His wife, Emily, and her young son Edward, managed to flee to nearby Krugersdorp, at least with some of the Hartley family paintings and artifacts before they too were consumed by British Imperial Forces' flames. One of those paintings by Thomas Baines was the "Giraffe Wearied" with the white-bearded Henry Hartley chasing the animal on horseback in the background.

Painting of "Giraffe Wearied" by Thomas Baines given to Henry Hartley, handled down to descendants of Henry Hartley and then gifted to the Southern Rhodesian Archives – now the Zimbabwe Archives[1]

[1] Image courtesy of Anne-Marie Moore (neé Hartley) – a direct descendent of Frederick Hartley. Inscription written on the back: "Presented to H. Hartley Esq. in acknowledgement of his kind assistance to the South African Goldfields Expedition by the artist, T. Baines, Gamyana River, Lat. 17.44.41. Sept. 14 1869". From left to right: Hartley's coloured servant Christiaan, Henry Hartley on Camelback and Baines following. The painting was in the possession of Mrs Joyce Hartley Theron of Johannesburg; it has been bequeathed to the National Archives by the late Mrs Gladys Hartley, but will remain in the custody of her three children during their lifetime. (see back cover)

Emily and her son, Edward, returned to *Thorndale* after hostilities ended. *Thorndale* is situated near the town of Magaliesberg where the Rhodesian railway line crossed the ox-wagon track (and now the main road) from Krugersdorp to Rustenburg. There is a pub there called Hartley's. It was eventually sold to a third party by Edward's not much liked wife, Maud Morgan, after his death.

As a young Boy Scout in the late 1950s and early 1960s I attended Scout Camps in Ladysmith and Mafeking was taken on conducted tours of the old Anglo-Boer War battlements. In the initial stages of the conflict the Boers ran rings around the vastly numerically superior and outfitted British Army. Baden-Powell was the commander of the garrison under siege at Mafeking and later founded the international Boy Scout Movement. The summer of 1899 was particularly wet with continuous thunderstorms that drenched the Brits and their equipment. They were ill prepared for the South African veld. They became bogged down and were easy targets for the much more agile ragtag Boers in loose commando-style, cavalry formations roaming the mountains, poorts and neks to close off any advancement towards the Transvaal. Ladysmith was besieged for 118 days, much to the embarrassment of Whitehall. Sadly, the battlements are mostly destroyed today by urban redevelopment or by vandalism. The Afrikaners – who eventually lost that definitive Second Anglo-Boer War against Imperial Britain – did not have much interest in preservation during Union. Nor does the current ANC government have much interest in the "white man's war".

There is an interesting coincidence between Henry **Hartley**, his third wife, Mary **Maloney**, and the past Prime Minister of South Africa, Hendrik **Verwoerd**.

Maloney's Eye farm, adjoining *Thorndale* farm, has a strong permanent spring. It was once owned by Mary Maloney (née Rorke), a young widow of only 22 years of age when she lost her husband. She had two young Maloney children when she married Henry Hartley in 1860 – also a widower at the time. This was his third marriage.

Hendrik Verwoerd was born in Amsterdam in the Netherlands before he moved with his devout Dutch Calvinist parents to Bulawayo Rhodesia in 1912 at the age of eleven. He attended Milton College Boys' School in Bulawayo. A bright student, he was awarded the very generous Beit Scholarship, sponsored by Jewish diamond magnet and financier Alfred Beit, on graduation at fourteen years of age. He could have studied at Oxford University under a subsequent equally-generous Abe Bailey Scholarship, but chose German universities at which to study.

Hendrik Verwoerd was an anti-Semitic, anti-British capitalist, anti-Catholic and anti-English. He wrote an academic paper entitled "Possible Solution to the Jewish Question in South Africa" in 1937. He was the chief architect of Apartheid in the mid-1950s, and a member of the exclusive Afrikaner Broederbond secret organization. He closed down all missionary schools for blacks in 1953 in favour of more universal, but inferior, "Bantu Education" that subjugated the black population to providing mainly manual labour from the native reserves to the minority white population.

His legacy is one of ethnic intolerance, separate development, racial segregation, the establishment of insular tribal Bantustans, and institutionalized white Afrikaner supremacy. He was an ardent Calvinist, not unlike Paul Kruger, a generation before him.

It was David Pratt – the English-speaking dairy farm owner of *Maloney's Eye* farm in the 1950s[1] who shot Hendrik Verwoerd point blank twice in the head, with a 0.22mm light pistol at the Rand Easter Show on April 9, 1960. Verwoerd survived the assassination attempt, recovered very quickly after surgery to lead the Afrikaner Nationalist Party to yet another election victory in 1961, and became a "revered" Apartheid hero until the transfer of majority rule to the ANC on April 26, 1994. On September 6, 1966, a second assassination attempt by a knife-wielding, Legislative Messenger, inside parliament, was fatal.

Favourite third son, Willie, died of black-water fever while hunting elephant (1853–1870)

Young Willie, was invincible on horseback pursuing elephants through the bush – like his father.

When Henry Hartley arrived at their Hartley Hills hunting and gold quartz exploration ox-wagon outpost on August 20, 1870 he was naturally distraught and distressed by the shocking, unexpected news.

He penned the following letter to his eldest son, Frederick, on the same day he learned for the very first time that his seventeen year-old, third-born son, Willie, had succumbed to fever and had died in the bush three months earlier while hunting elephants. (There were no mobile cellular phones in those days.)

---

[1] Originally owned by Boer Generaal "Koos" (A.J.G.) de la Rey and transferred to Thomas William Maloney on December 5, 1876.

Umvoolie August 20, 1870

My dear Frederick

It is with painful feelings I write to inform you that your poor dear brother Willie is no more. He died the 29th May on a little spruit between Inloondas and Umvoolie. You cannot judge of my feelings. I loved you all equally, there is no difference in my heart and there was none to spare, but God willed it otherwise and has taken him away and I hope to a better place.

Although you have estranged yourself from me I love you with a father's fond affection and it has been a source of great grief to me. I went with Mr. Leask to see where they had laid him down to his last rest, accompanied by Mr. Baines and Jewell, and Mr. Baines has taken a sketch of his grave. I shall ever remember Mr. Leask's kindness with gratitude. Poor Tom went down with fever at the same time and the young man who was with him died the night after him. Everyone have been down with fever but Mr. Leask, and in consequence of sickness nothing has been done.

I shall commence my homeward route in about ten days or a fortnight at the fatherest and hope, if I live to return, that we shall be more united. It has not been my fault, I have done a little but not much, and I have no more heart to hunt for I miss him in the field as well as camp and I feel lost. Give my love to Sarah.

May God bless you in the earnest prayer of your bereaved father.

H. Hartley.

No doubt this letter, in Henry's beautiful quill-pen cursive handwriting, still preserved today, was immediately handed to a post office carrier for delivery to his eldest son Frederick in the Magaliesberg, on horseback and by runners.

It tells us much of Henry Hartley's feelings, mind-set, character, personality traits, personal relationships and love for his sons. Also, a reluctance to immediately forgive his serious disagreements with his eldest son, or to accept blame for the estrangement.

Frederick was 26 years old at the time and probably beginning to exert his own independence from his strict, disciplined father. He was becoming a very successful coffee, tobacco and citrus farmer in his own right on his own farms in the Magaliesberg. He was married, settled and the young father of four children himself. It is also clear that Frederick was not part of the hunting trip in August 1870.

The estrangement must have happened during the period when Hartley was recovering on his farm, after his near fatal encounter with a rhinoceros in November 1969.

There must have been some sort of a reconciliation between father and son, because Frederick accompanied his dad, Thomas Baines, his 10 year-old half-brother "Harry" and his stepmother on a hunting and expedition trip looking for diamondiferous pipes in June and July of 1871 to the Tati gold diggings (at present-day Francistown, Botswana). Frederick also lent Baines six oxen for his ox-wagon trip to meet again with Chief Lobengula.

(A copy of the letter, with the black ink rather faded now, is included in the Appendices at the end of this biography. It was kindly provided to me by Ann-Marie Moore (neé Hartley), a direct descendant of Frederick – now living in Johannesburg).

That letter must be one of the only letters in existence written in the hand of Henry Hartley himself.

T.V. Bulpin in his historic account *To the Banks of the Zambezi* (1965) on page 168 writes that . . .

> William Hartley, the favourite son of old Hartley, was another headstrong hunter who stated boldly that he was not afraid of fever and would pursue elephants wherever they were to be found. He died on 29th May of that year (1870) with his name and the date of his death carved on the trunk of the tree which gave the shade to the antelopes who wandered across his grave. (*probably from black-water fever*). His hunting companion, James O'Donnell, died on the same day and was buried a couple of miles away. Henry McGillewie also found the mosquitoes more deadly foes than elephants that year and came to the end of the trail in the bush.
>
> Old Hartley, with the wisdom of the years, arrived at leisure on the 20th August and was horrified to hear of the death of his son and all the other hunters. The old man was limping badly from his crushed leg and his shaking from the rhino. He stayed with (Thomas) Baines, and was a subdued individual compared to his former self, brooding over his son's grave and pottering about prospecting rather than resuming his full zest for hunting.[1]

---

[1] Hartley also brought news that dissident regiments of the deceased Zulu King/Chief Mzilikazi had been overwhelmed by those in favour of his designated successor Chief Lobengula; that there were rumours that the *South African Gold Fields Exploration Company* was going out of business and that Baines's competent Swedish mineralogist and mining engineer, Mr Nelson, from the previous year had failed to return to Hartley Hills as expected with Henry Hartley, and was reported to have sailed back to Europe.

Henry Hartley did not forget his blacksmith trade as a professional elephant hunter, nor his desire to help out his friends in need. Thomas Leask in his diary entry for August 23, 1870 reports: "Mr Hartley welded my waggon tyre (wheel rim) and I made a new disselboom, so that the waggon is set up again". This was on the same day that Hartley arrived back by horse to his Hartley Hills outpost in Matabeleland from the Transvaal. He learned for the very first time the devastating news that his youngest son Willie Hartley (17) had died three months earlier of black-water fever. After going down to the lowveld "fly" country where elephants were more prolific, all members of the hunting party had become very ill and seven of the party had succumbed to fever. But Hartley had time to fire up his blacksmith forge and goatskin bellows to manufacture and fit a new tempered wheel rim for Leask, before going to visit the gravesite, 22 miles away. "William, a young man, was full of hope and strength, while the old [man] was weak and emaciated, with three broken ribs which he got by a toss from a rhinoceros, and to-day age and white hairs are weeping at the grave of youth . . . For his son's sake the old man, tho' still weak came in this year . . . "[1]

Fourth son Henry ("Harry") Albert Rorke (by a third marriage)

Like his famous father, "Harry" was an accomplished horseman from a very young age. He also had an exuberant, fearless and mischievous nature.

He was only 13 when his mother died and 14 when his father died. His father had arranged for Harry to attend residential boarding school in the Natal Colony.[2] After just nine months the school funds ran out. At the age of 17, while still in Natal, he was conscripted to fight against the Zulus.

Napoléon, the exiled Bonaparte Prince Imperial and only child of Napoleon III, Emperor of France, volunteered to fight in the Anglo-Zulu War with the British 17th Lancers. A proficient horseman himself, he and a small reconnaissance party – that included Harry – had dismounted so that the Prince could make some sketches of the terrain, and were ambushed by a group of Zulu impis on June 1, 1879. The Prince was speared to death numerous times with assegais. Harry managed to escape the ambush on his horse, and fought in the Battle of Isandlawanda. Harry was one of only four soldiers to survive that significant battle.[3]

---

[1] Leask, Thomas, *Southern African Diaries of 1865–1870*, edited by Wallis, 1954, pp. 212 & 213

[2] Berrington, Aileen, 1987, p. 218

[3] Berrington, Aileen, 1987, p. 219. According to Britishbattles.com around 60 Europeans survived the battle.

After the Anglo-Zulu War he went to live with his older stepbrother Tom Maloney at his *Maloney's Eye* farm next to *Thorndale* and went into business with him as an ox-wagon transporter between Pietermaritzburg and Krugersdorp.

He served with the British in 1881 at the Battle of Majuba in the First Anglo-Boer War.

He was conscripted to fight with the local Boer commandos at the start of the Second Anglo-Boer War in 1899, and was next to his older half-brother, Thomas John, when Thomas John was killed at Pieter's Hill outside Colenso, also fighting with the Boers.

After that decisive second civil war Harry was employed by British forces in charge of military ox-wagon convoys. He was called to service again during the 1914 mine workers' rebellion for the new South African Union government under Prime Minister Louis Botha.

Harry Rorke inherited the irreplaceable Hartley Family Bible from 1846 – an heirloom still in the family possession.

Chapter 20:

Current Hartley generation still farming in the Magaliesberg

Henry Hartley (the big game hunter) is Simon Hartley's (b. 1968) paternal grandfather's grandfather. In order of lineage: Henry Hartley, Henry ("Harry") Albert Rouke, then Charles Henry, and Henry Charles – Simon's dad.

Henry Charles Hartley (June 10, 1932–April 20, 2020) bought a small 22ha farm located about 10km west of Rustenburg, situated against the Magaliesberg mountains – not too distant from the original *Thorndale* farm – called *Rain Hill* in 1978 from the McGregor family. Simon and his family have lived there ever since. In 2003 he and his wife, Adele, bought the farm from his dad, where they raised their three children, Sarah, Oliver and Emily.

Simon grows and roasts coffee as a hobby, experiments and grows a variety of citrus and avocadoes, has a farm stall, and a restaurant called "Hartleys" operated by Simon's elder brother Michael since 1999. It closed during the Covid-19 pandemic. He still runs an accommodation business, especially for wedding events. The wedding chapel is able to seat 120 guests.

Simon gives demonstrations on his coffee growing and roasting hobby at his *Rain Hill* farm. Dinners are often provided in the large citrus packing shed, which has a wonderful atmosphere. It was a pub and restaurant with music bands for many years before Covid-19 hit. The current Hartley family also ran a very nice Saturday country market for fresh organic products for many years, always donating the entrance fees to charity. The farm is adjacent to the Kloof Resort with its beautiful natural rock pools, waterfalls, views, and a climb up through the gorge to the plateau on the top of the mountain – now known as the Kwagswane Nature Reserve – on what was previously a Paul Kruger-owned farm.

In 2022 Simon and his family no longer grow tobacco or hunt for elephants and rhino, like their grandfather's grandfather and his four sons, Frederick, Tom, Willie and "Harry"!

Henry Charles (nearly 88) died unexpectedly of a heart attack on April 20, 2020 while on an extended holiday to Sweden, on the night before he and his travelling companion were scheduled to fly home to RSA. President Cyril Ramaphosa was intending to impose severe international travel restrictions in the wake of the Covid-19 pandemic at the time. Cyril announced the very strict "total" lockdown of South Africa on March 23, 2020, and it went into effect on March 27, 2020.

Henry Charles was a well-established, and well-liked Pharmacist in Rustenburg with two dispensaries, and was a part-time farmer. He served as a Town Councillor twice and as Deputy Mayor of Rustenburg Municipality once.

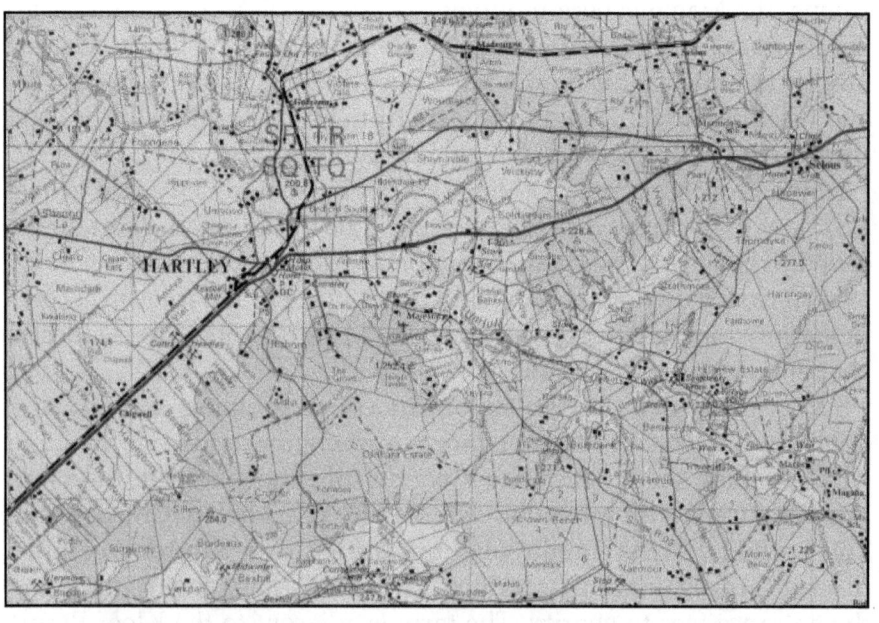

Extract of 1:250,000 Topo-cadastral Map of Hartley Town
– published by the Surveyor General, Rhodesia, 1974
(courtesy of Michael Tucker)

Chapter 21:

Founder of the town of Hartley & Hartley Hills in central Zimbabwe (Rhodesia)

"In the 1980s a family member by the name of Aileen Berrington set about collecting the Hartley family stories and history and put it together"[1] in a detailed genealogical format. This was in the days before word processing on computers, and the manuscript was laboriously typed up on single sheets of legal size paper with corrections using white typex. Simon Hartley (b. 1968) scanned a copy of the 240 page manuscript to share with other family members in an attempt to preserve its existence from rot and fish moths. A treasure trove of information on the early days of Henry Hartley, his parents, siblings and considerable offspring is contained in that manuscript.

Simon and his son, Oliver Hartley, visited Chigutu (formerly Hartley) and Hartley Hills in Zimbabwe en route to Malawi in 2013. The current Hartley generation were fortunate to meet up with some very enthusiastic local folks, in particular the headmaster of Bryden College, Howard Matthews, who was well versed in the local history thanks to all his research. Howard and his wife showed them the town and also took Simon and Oliver to Hartley Hills where they still dig for gold and where a plaque was unveiled in 1969, but sadly has been badly vandalised.[2] Simon is also in possession of the family bible given by Henry Hartley to his youngest and fourth son "Harry" that dates to 1846. Simon intends to "traipse around" the ancestral *Thorndale* farm when he next visits Magaliesberg to find the grave site of his famous ancestor Henry Hartley.

---

[1] E-mail from Simon Hartley dated November 9, 2020. Berrington, Aileen, 1987
[2] Copy of the "Programme for celebrating Henry Hartley's Hill on 28th September 1969" on the 100th anniversary of the founding of the settlement.

Chapter 22:
Concluding Commentary

Philosophy and years ahead of their time in a pre-colonial era, and their legacy

Within the context of the mid 1800s, Hartley and Baines were non-racist in their attitudes to the bantu tribesmen and aboriginal peoples with whom they engaged. They carefully respected their very different cultures, and tribal hierarchies. They diligently adhered to verbal agreements made with the paramount chiefs. Hartley was fully fluent in their languages. He thoroughly understood "Matabele and Mashona etiquette". There was considerable trust between the dichotomy of almost opposite cultures. Hartley and Baines were not colonialists themselves. This was pre-colonial contact for mutual benefit between whites and blacks in this Northern Ndebele/Zulu kingdom, north of the Afrikaner-ruled Transvaal Republiek.

They were active in their communities and attended traditional church services with their families. There are several specific reported instances in the diaries where Thomas Baines and Henry Hartley attended religious services together with all the local tribesmen at Missionary Stations on Sundays in Matabeleland; and then had a separate service later in the day with the missionaries, their wives and children, to be amongst their own comrades and countrymen. Afterwards a meal was generally shared within their own culture.

Henry Hartley, in particular, was an excellent observer in understanding people. He internalized how Matabele society worked. They sat around the warm campfires on chilly nights while outspanned, even with the lowest echelon of servants – unless a particular individual was being ostracized for unbecoming behaviour. They drank native sorghum beer and ate with members of the Royal Kraals. Hartley was even present at the death bed of King Mzilikazi on September 5, 1868 and read verses from the bible to him.

It was not uncommon for a warrior husband in the 1800s to severely beat his wife (or wives) for almost no apparent reason (from a European perspective) in that gender-subjugated Matabele society. Female hierarchy in tribal society was restricted to domestic chores, raising children, carrying water and firewood to the family kraal and hewing in the fields. The men looked after the cattle and hunted or trained as warriors.

Corporal punishment was commonly practised in the Victorian era by both Europeans and Africans. It was not unusual for a father to cane his son for "disobedience", irrespective of race. Corporal punishment by teachers was even accepted practice in British residential boarding schools and other educational settings up to the 1970s.

We have, fortunately, moved a long way from the Victorian era of prejudicial racial and gender bias, and corporal punishment.

Although colonialism had reached the eastern Cape Colony – then known as British Kaffraria – as well as the Orange Free State, southern Natal, and the ZAR Transvaal Republiek, it had not yet reached the northern parts of southern Africa, where the local tribes and chieftains were still very much in control of their territories. (The exiled Zulu Chief Mzilikazi was, of course, a colonist himself when his tribe invaded and settled Matabeleland in the 1840s). White traders, big-game hunters and mineral prospectors needed to have the consent of the local chieftain before they were permitted to hunt or obtain a mining concession.

Yet, looking back 150 years, what was Henry Hartley's legacy when evaluating the impact he had on "harmless" wildlife wondering the southern continent of Africa, relatively contently and peacefully in natural balance.

The deadly two-bore elephant gun was the game changer that he and his fellow hunters, both black and white, pursued in hunting elephants and rhinos for their valuable ivory to virtual extinction; This occurred firstly in the Cape Colony beyond Grahamstown, and then progressively northwards, through the Transvaal, Bechuanaland and present-day Zimbabwe towards the Zambezi River. Environmental sustainability and stewardship was not something that they understood. Hartley did understand short-term profit!

Ironically, it was the belligerent Paul Kruger who left a wildlife legacy. As President of the Transvaal Republic he realized that wildlife in the Zuid Afrikaaanse Republiek was rapidly being desecrated, and initiated the establishment of wildlife sanctuaries along the eastern boundaries of the country. His Volksraad did not initially support his vision.[1] Today the Kruger National Park, together with private game reserves to the west and the adjacent *Parque Naçional Do Limpopo* to the east, in Moçambique at 99,800km^2, is one of the largest game sanctuaries in the world. This is nearly five times the size of the Kruger National Park. Named the *Great Limpopo Transfrontier Park* there is free movement for wildlife across the international border and between the public and private game reserves.

[1] Carruthers, Jane, 1995, *The Kruger National Park: A Social and Political History.* Pietermaritzburg: University of Natal Press, p. 15

Chapter 23:

Postscript

There appears to be a consistent five-stage evolution of pre-colonialism in the 1700s to post-colonialism in the 2020s. This seems to apply everywhere in the Old and New Worlds, differing only by degree.

In the "Age of Misinformation", I have tried to be on the ground with Henry Hartley and his contemporaries in his ox-wagon and on his horse, experiencing what they experienced. I wish to remain true to the facts, gleaned from hand-written 1800's field notes, original primary documents and sources, and avoid speculation and exaggeration. Thomas Baines (1820-1875) was particularly articulate, open and honest in his reporting.

While writing this biography I became intrigued in using comparative history of colonialism across countries from the "Age of Enlightenment" in the 1700s to today. It divides colonialism into five definitive phases, and seems to be universal, rather than being particularly limited to southern Africa:

Phase 1: Pre-colonial initial contact with mutually acceptable trade between European explorers and indigenous groups. Both willing buyers and willing sellers achieving fair market value in the free exchange by both parties

Phase 2: Colonial "invasions" and European settlement in the new world; and hostile annihilations

Phase 3: Independence of colonial rule

Phase 4: Post-colonial apologists and cancel culture movements

Phase 5: Recolonization of independent countries by foreign powers other than Europeans.

Phase 1: Pre-colonial initial contact between European Explorers and indigenous groups

Much of this short period of contact was typified by pleasantries and productive contacts between the explorers and tribes, exchanges of gifts and the granting of hunting and mineral exploration concessions.

This is particularly reflected in the period of 1840 to about the 1870s when Thomas Baines and Henry Hartley and his fellow adventurers were roaming around the future Rhodesia/Zimbabwe hunting elephants for their ivory and prospecting for gold under the auspices of the exiled Ndebele/Zulu King and his indunas.

When the young 15-year-old John Ross travelled overland through Zululand to Delegoa Bay to obtain much needed medical supplies for the British settlement at Port Natal in 1825, King Shaka Zulu was most impressed by the bravery shown by the young boy and assisted him on his mission.

When Captain James Cook landed at Nootka Sound in 1778 on the coast of British Columbia in Canada he called it "Friendly Cove", because the local population were mostly peaceful and welcoming of European sailors. They traded beaver pelts, which were plentiful, for six-inch iron nails to forge into tempered steel implements and weapons.

There is so little known, recorded or taught of pre-colonial British Columbia history. The only record that I have come across is John R. Jewett's personal account of the local culture around 1790 at Nootka Sound. No different to what Shaka Zulu, Mzilikazi, Lobengula, or even Paul Kruger (in at least one instance recorded by David Livingstone) did to defeated enemy tribes; i.e. After killing all the enemy men, they took over their surviving women and children as slaves or indentured servants.

Most of the Crown land in the Province of British Columbia is still unceded territory, where resource, cultural and land ownership issues in unceded territories of multiple overlapping indigenous clans remain unresolved today.

This is unlike the comprehensive *Treaty of Waitangi* in New Zealand, widely signed by most parties on February 6, 1840, which resolved opposing political and land ownership issues at the time, between the British Crown and the Māori population during the European colonization period.

The Māoris sailed from Polynesia and colonized/settled New Zealand from around 1300 AD. They exterminated/assimilated the earlier indigenous Moriori people.[1] This was colonization/invasion of other people during the pre-colonial European era.

The 1700s were also the "Age of Enlightenment" of Captain James Cook and Captain Vancouver, exploring Australasia and the Pacific West Coast of North America, and sharing their geographic knowledge with everyone.

---

[1] As an aside, the large flightless indigenous bird, the Moa, which reached 3.6m in height and 230kg in weight – and a good source of meat – became extinct around that period.

Phase 2: Colonial "invasions" and European settlement in the new world

The earlier Spanish Conquests to Central, and South America and Mexico in the 1500s were very different, exterminating most of the indigenous peoples they encountered, and destroying their civilizations.

In Africa this period started with the Portuguese and Dutch sea voyages around the southern tip of Africa to trade with India and the Far East in the 1400s to 1600s. There were no proper safe harbours along the South African coastline, except at Delagoa Bay, and the local warrior tribes were not welcoming.

Only in the 1700s did European colonial settlement and the "Scramble for Africa" begin in earnest, peaking in 1885 when the Berlin Convention carved up and distributed the entire African continent amongst the European powers.

See in particular the "Map of Africa, South of the Equator", included in the Appendices. It shows the dates and colonial boundaries decided upon at that Convention or soon afterwards. Incredibly, country boundaries have not changed much since 1885 (unlike Europe and the Soviet Union).

This Phase 2 also includes the missionary period when Christian missionaries were sent to remote parts of the world to baptise and educate the "barbaric" heathens.

European colonialism did follow later, including Matabeleland and Mashonaland in what became known as Rhodesia. This was long after the death of our two esteemed gentlemen, Henry Hartley and Thomas Baines. The negative change in racial attitudes only occurred with the arrival of Cecil John Rhodes in the 1890s when he took over the land between the Limpopo and Zambezi rivers for the benefit of Imperialist British settlers with allegiance to Queen Victoria. Under his direction the local inhabitants were "slaughtered".

With the help of Mashona and other previously subjugated tribes, Cecil John Rhodes used newly-invented Maxim machine guns to mow down Matabele warrior assegai throwing tribesmen (albeit some with breech-loading rifles that they were unaccustomed to firing) at Bulawayo, in their tens of thousands, including women and children. They sprinkled their shields "with medicine to render them assegai and bulletproof and to make the warriors themselves invincible in battle . . ."[1] It did not work!

---

[1] Baines, Thomas, *Diaries of 1869–1872*, edited by Wallis, 1946

"In Southern Africa, history is not a set of neutrally observed and agreed-upon facts: present concerns colour interpretations of even the remote past. For all the contestants in contemporary Southern Africa there has been a conscious struggle to control the past in order to legitimate the present and lay claim to the future. Who is telling what history for which Africa is a question that needs constantly to be addressed.[1]

Rhodes' dictum in the late 1870s was "Equal rights for all civilized men" . . . where merit, and not colour, should be the test of political and economic advancement". "One man, one vote" became the dictum of black liberation movements in the 1950s.

Rethinking the way even recent history is interpreted is not all a black-and-white, bare-bone, structured recording of actual historic facts. Each observer examining those "facts" will colour in their own interpretations of reality in the past – and even the present.

Sadly, there seems to be so much misinformation, and even deliberate disinformation, spread on the Internet and in the mass media today on what is reality and what is fiction!

Emmerson Mnangagwa was a lieutenant in Robert Mugabe's Zimbabwean government in the 1980s. He took over power from the aging septuagenarian in a military coup in 2017. Mnangagwa continues to try to control the narrative of Zimbabwean history with "cancel culture" tactics, by removing memorial plaques of victims of the genocide that he perpetrated against the mostly Matabele-speaking supporters of Joshua Nkomo in the post-independence period.

> An estimated 20,000 civilians were killed from 1983 to 1987 in a campaign by the Zimbabwean army's notorious (North-Korean trained) Fifth Brigade, targeting dissidents in the Matebeleland region, an opposition stronghold. The military operation became known as Gukurahundi – "the rain that washes away the chaff."[2]

Sadly, genocide is not an unknown phenomenon in southern Africa, even associated with the European colonization era.

> About 65,000 Herero people and about 10,000 Nama people died in the German military onslaught from 1904 to 1908 in the country now known as Namibia, after an uprising by those who had lost their land and livestock to the colonial authorities. . .

---

[1] *Encyclopedia Britannica* published September 30, 2020. www.britannica.com/place/Southern Africa. Access date: May 21, 2021
[2] York, Geoffrey, & Moya, Jeffery, *The Globe & Mail* newspaper of January 12, 2022, p. A15

It began with an extermination order from a German commander, vowing to destroy the Herero people, who had rebelled against German colonial rule in South West Africa.

"That nation must vanish from the face of the Earth", General Lother Von Trother told his soldiers in 1904 as they forced people into the desert to starve. Tens of thousands soon perished from bullets, hunger, thirst, or slave labour in concentration camps.[1]

The British were guilty of genocide when they forced thousands of Boer women and children, and their black servants out of their farm homesteads into concentration camps to be housed in canvas tents on the cold winter veld. Contagious diseases spread rapidly amongst the incarcerated. This was after the Transvaal capital Pretoria had quickly fallen to Lord Roberts' troops in 1900. At the end of formal hostilities of the Anglo-Boer War at the Peace of Vereeniging on May 31, 1902, *bittereinde* menfolk refused to give up fighting, but continued to use hit-and-run guerrilla tactics. About 25,000 Afrikaners plus 12,000 bantu servants perished, most notably at the Bethule Concentration Camp on the Orange River border with the Cape Colony.[2] About 20,000 of the Afrikaner losses were women and children,[3] 22,000 British soldiers and their white colonial allies also lost their lives in that unnecessary conflict. Imagine what a different South Africa would have been without these terrible losses in human life.

It is interesting to compare the distribution of population in the Cape Colony of 1865 with the same regions in 2019.

Population in Western and Eastern Cape – racial breakdown between 1865 and 2019 . . .

Population by race in March 1865 . . [4]

Race	Western Cape Colony		Eastern Cape Colony	
	Population March 1865	%	Population March 1865	%
Europeans	105,358	45%	76,244	29%
"Hottentots"	52,637	22%	28,961	11%
"Kaffirs"	9,176	4%	91,360	35%
Not classed	69,139	29%	63,516	24%
Total	**236,300**	**100%**	**260,081**	**100%**

[1] York, Geoffrey, *The Globe & Mail* newspaper of May 29, 2021, p. 11.
[2] The Bethule Concentration Camp had a particularly high death rate. Reference: Van Zÿl, Jan, "Bethule 1896-1907, met spesifieke verwysing na die Anglo-Boeroolog". Doctoral Thesis, Universiteit van die Vrystaat, November, 2019, Bloemfontein
[3] Kanfer, Stephen, 1993, p. 151
[4] Algar, Frederick, *The Diamond Fields: with notes on the Cape Colony and Natal, 1872*, p. 20, quoting official census for 1865; and Statistics South Africa for mid-year population estimates for 2019

Population by race in mid 2019 ... [1]				
White	1,095,084	16%	315,477	5%
Coloured	3,422,136	50%	563,831	8%
Black African	2,258,610	33%	5,799,406	86%
Indian/Asian	68,443	1%	33,561	1%
Total	**6,844,272**	**100%**	**6,712,276**	**100%**

The Cape Colony Census for March 1865 also tabulated the number of horses, cattle and other livestock for each district, morgen[2] under cultivation and agricultural products produced.

Although the population in absolute numbers has increased substantially since 1865, the proportion of black Africans in the Eastern Cape increased from 35% to 86%, and the proportion of whites decreased from 29% to 5% over the same period.

Phase 3: Independence of colonial rule

In Africa this period commenced in earnest in the waning years of the British Empire following 1945. The British were exhausted after winning the Second World War.

It was exemplified by Harold MacMillan's "Winds of Change Speech" to the South African white-only parliament on February 3, 1960, shortly before the first assassination attempt was made on the life of the Prime Minister, Hendrik Verwoerd, by David Pratt from *Maloney's Eye* dairy farm next to *Thorndale* farm in the Magaliesberg.

A flurry of European colonies gained full independence from their former European overseers from 1960, except for minority, white-ruled Southern Africa. Majority-rule only arrived in Rhodesia in 1980, Namibia in 1989 and in South Africa in 1994.

Ian Smith revived "divide and rule" predispositions between the sparring Matabele and Mashona tribes and kept control even with a minority of no more than 240,000 white settlers, in a country of 4.5 million people. Millions of citizens left Zimbabwe post-independence with the economic collapse and corruption of Robert Mugabe's increasingly despotic régime.

But, "it is the exception that proves the rule". Despite all the political chaos around it, Botswana has succeeded for decades as a democratic, peaceful country. Instead of incurring unsustainable debt, corruption and rioting, it has invested its diamond mining windfall from the Orapa diamondiferous pipes (discovered on the edge of the Kalahari desert in the 1970s) for the benefit of present and future

---

[1] Proportion of population by race for 2019 update – derived from 2011 census percentages
[2] A Cape-Dutch survey land area measurement, equivalent to 2.12 English acres.

generations – like Norway has done with its oil windfall and Sovereign Fund; and which Alberta and Nigeria have blown away and misspent. The Orapa diamond mine is jointly owned and operated by the government and the international De Beers Consolidated Mines Limited (Anglo American Corporation PLC) for the long term. Rough diamonds are cut and polished by highly-trained locals in Gaborone rather than in Antwerp in Belgium. As a desert country it protects its precious wildlife to promote a lucrative tourism industry for its people. It also has a successful cattle industry.

Formerly known as the Bechuanaland Protectorate, within the British Sphere of Influence, during the lifetime of Henry Hartley, it was one of the poorest and least developed countries on the continent, prior to full independence in 1966. It is one of the few countries in Africa, or the world for that matter, that function as a true stable democracy.

Botswana with its relatively small homogeneous Tswana-speaking people have an historic culture of consultation amongst the chieftains-in-council where the peoples' problems have to be listened to and addressed. Elected politicians drive around in ordinary pickup trucks serving their constituents, rather than in fancy Mercedes Benz luxury sedans roaming the country for graft and corruption. There is relatively little corruption in government, and, unlike South Africa, there appears to be almost no looting of the public purse.

Phase 4: Post-colonial apologists, and "cancel culture" movements

This is a very recent phenomenon exacerbated by the terrible murder of George Floyd in 2020 in the USA during the "I cannot breathe" global Covid-19 pandemic; and the emergence of wokism and the cancel culture movement of the Critical Race Theory era, by labelling old white European men as the evil perpetrators of colonialism. It calls for the rewriting of history.

It ignores the atrocities that occurred between local indigenous tribal societies during the pre-colonial periods and plays down positive changes and impacts of good governance during the Age of Enlightenment and the European colonial period. It forgets that we are a global village today with instantaneous communication via the Internet, and where free trade is mutually beneficial.

With little regard to the historic facts we are fed anti-colonial, racially-charged, and revisionist populism by our mass media. We rarely hear of the non-racist, conciliatory and integrationist philosophies of Martin Luther King, Nelson Mandela or Bishop Tutu. They have been forgotten.

In my opinion, divisive politics is ruining nations and civil societies.

The practice of "cancelling" people because their views are deemed to be offensive by some, or of denying them a platform to speak, has become a subject of heated debate.

That is why I loved reading *Extraordinary Popular Delusions & The Madness of Crowds* authored by Charles Mackay in 1841 – also nearly two hundred years ahead of its time.

The attempted Insurrection by extremist supporters of Donald J. Trump in Washington DC on January 6, 2021, against Joe Biden and the Democratic Party; and the attempted insurrection by former President Jacob Zuma on July 15, 2021 in Durban Kwa-Zulu/Natal against Cyril Ramaphosa, seem to replicate the American Civil War and the Afrikaner/Krugerism and Shaka/Zulu domination of the 1800s.

Both insurrection attempts failed. Democracy prevailed.

Phase 5: Recolonization of independent countries by foreign powers other than Europeans.

The recent invasion and attempted recolonization of independent Ukraine[1] is a case in point.

Another disturbing trend of recolonization is emerging, perpetrated by President-for-Life Jinping Xi and his CCP comrades in Beijing.

First stop, Africa and the Africans. Hong Kong, Taiwan and then who knows where?

He does not need to invade Africa. He already "owns" that continent. Demography is working against his communist regime with its aging population.

China's population is expected to reach a peak of 1.410 million by 2029 (in just 7 years' time) and then stagnate like many first-world countries, because of its decades-old one-child policy, previous affinity for female infanticide, and declining fertility.

31% of the population is currently in the 20-year-old to 39-year-old age bracket, in the prime of their working years and ability to fight a conventional war. By 2050 one-third of its population will be over 60 years old, and perhaps older with declining morbidity and preference for very small families. Immigration and multi-cultural diversity is not encouraged. There is no democratic freedom. No independent judicial system. Execution. A rigid draconian society. No unrestricted access to the Internet. Robotic compliance with authority. No trade unions.

Google and *Facebook* and *Twitter* accounts are banned in China.

---

[1] The size of Texas.

Now is the opportunity for China to be the most successful nation in world domination, and to secure the world's natural resources before it is too late.

And they have seized that opportunity.

The Chinese Communist Party government has effectively taken over the running and ownership of the new modernized Mombasa Port in Kenya and the new international airport in Lusaka, Zambia, because the governments in those countries defaulted on their infrastructure loans owed to the Chinese government-owned construction companies. In addition to granting substantial loans for infrastructure that incur unsustainable long-term debt, Chinese workers are entitled to settle in Zambia and Kenya at the end of their contracts as citizens, and start local businesses.

They have also built the massively-expensive Kazungula road and rail bridge across the Zambezi River at the intersection of the Zambia, Zimbabwe, Namibia Caprivi Strip and Botswana borders. It is 18.5m wide and 923m long, and will facilitate the export of copper, cobalt, chrome and other valuable commodities via Port Elizabeth to mainland China.

I have read that the Chinese government and its state-owned companies have accumulated over US$41 trillion in outstanding debt, which is equivalent to the size of the USA economy – and three times the size of the Chinese economy. The USA's outstanding debt is half that at around US$21 trillion, which is at an historic high because of tax breaks and pandemic spending, pushing the debt onto future generations of Americans.

But, China also has an enormous current trade surplus with their trading partners, accumulated over recent decades of super-normal GDP growth. The country has been able to collect a humongous stash of exchangeable US Dollars, to buy up the West and other emerging countries at will.

Is Chinese neo-colonialism of Africa any worse, or better than European colonization in past centuries? Time will tell.

The senseless unprovoked invasion of Ukraine, a democratic, independent, freedom-loving country, by Vladimir Putin and his confrontational régime in Moscow on February 22, 2022, is further evidence of this Phase 5. This follows his partly successful and unprovoked annexation of Crimea and eastern regions of Ukraine adjoining Russia, immediately after the Winter Sochi Games in 2014.

Using blitzkrieg terror, reminiscent of Hitler's horror tactics in the 1930s and 1940s during World War II, Russia bombed millions of innocent people in Ukraine with supersonic ballistic missiles, fighter jets, percussion bombs, and artillery fire. Thousands of armoured tanks and ground troops swept across from all directions that caused at least half of the 44 million population of Ukraine to be displaced, or to flee for their lives to Europe as refugees.

The horror of this war is hidden from the Russian people by disinformation, propaganda, blatant racism, and fear of the truth by the Russian régime. A desire on the part of Putin to recreate the Russian Czarist Empire of the 1700s and 1800s, and leave a "legacy" for himself?

At the time of writing, September 2022, the Russian War on Ukraine had not yet been resolved.

Appendices

- Extract from 1846 Hartley Family Bible showing important dates (Courtesy of the Hartley Family)
- Letter from David Livingstone to Thomas Baines, September 1858 (Extracted from Thomas Baines's Journal of 1877)
- Anxious letter from Henry Hartley sent to Thomas Baines from Hartley Hills on July 4th, 1869 (MS.049.5.48, The Brenthurst Library)
- Extract of rhino sketch and rivers from Thomas Baines's original field notes July 15, 1869 (MS 049/9.2, from page 90, The Brenthurst Library)
- Agreement of mining concession, August 1871 (Extracted from pages 695 and 696 of Thomas Baines's Diary)
- Copy of personal letter penned by Henry Hartley on August 20, 1870 on learning of the death of his third-born son, Willie, while elephant hunting near Hartley Hills (Courtesy of Ann-Marie Moore, neé Hartley)
- Exchange of correspondence relating to mining company formation i.e. Letter dated 23, October 1874 from Thomas Baines to Henry Hartley (MS.049.6.10, The Brenthurst Library)
- Map of South East African Gold Fields by Thomas Baines of his exploits to 1875
- Map of 1884 boundaries of colonial claims. "Africa South of the Equator" published in 1890 (Courtesy of www.RareMaps.com)
- Stanford's New Map of the Orange Free State and the southern part of the South African Republic, 1899, published by Edward Stanford, London, just before outbreak of the Second and deciding Anglo-Boer War – "The Crisis in South Africa" (Courtesy of Barry Ruderman of Barry Lawrence Ruderman Antique Maps Inc.)

Extract from 1846 Hartley Family Bible showing important dates
(Courtesy of the Hartley Family)

Facsimile of Letter from Dr Livingstone to Mr Thomas Baines

Senna, 19th Sept
1858

My Dear Baines

The Lynx entered the Kongone with some provisions and lots of correspondence. I sent up two officers who accompanied Dr Kirk to the shore stockade to beg four canoes to bring up what the Lynx had brought

Letter from David Livingstone to Thomas Baines, September 1858
(Extracted from Thomas Baines's Journal of 1877)

> Ingateen July 4. 1869
>
> T Baines Esq[r]
>
> My Dear Sir
>
> I fully expected you before this but hope you will not be long behind us lighten your waggons all you can and follow as quick as you can minding to keep my trek Sir John is here but intends starting tomorrow he has been trieing for a Monopoly he is all self and most illiberal in all his dealings of any one that I have come in contact with he also has stated that your party are intirely under his direction and had he known of your approach he should have sent to stop your further progress of course you know best and if he has that power why the gold fields will not be worked while he has or that the power is vested in him if I can possibly prevent it you know your authority and of course know what to do this of course is strictly Confidential,
>
> best regards to all our friends
>
> I remain
> My Dear Sir
> Yours Truly
> H Hartley

Anxious letter from Henry Hartley sent to Thomas Baines from Hartley Hills on July 4th, 1869 (MS.049.5.48, The Brenthurst Library)

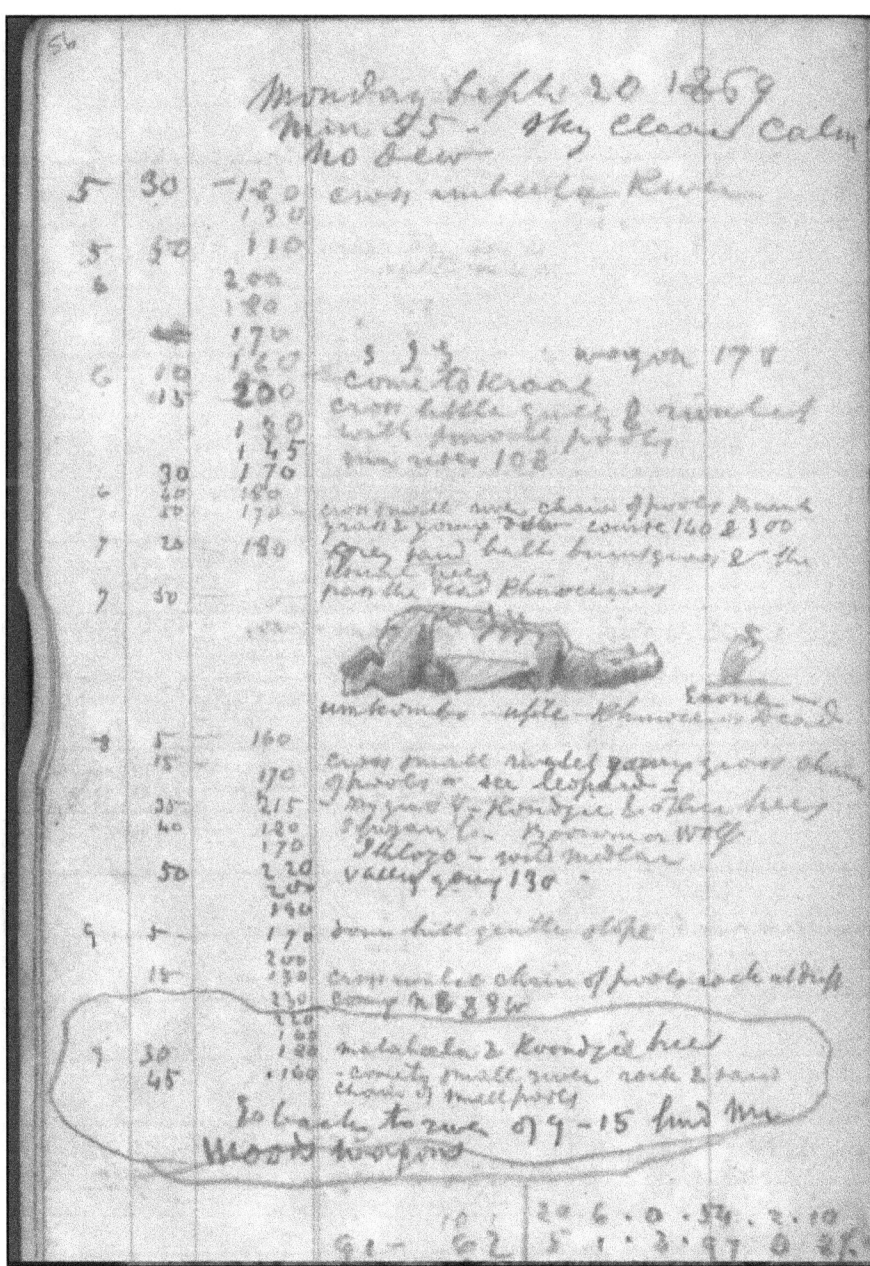

Extract of rhino sketch and rivers from Thomas Baines's original field notes July 15, 1869 (MS 049/9.2, from page 90, The Brenthurst Library)

to sign them all, including the grant of mining rights to me. I had already drawn this out in the form of a confirmation of the original verbal grant and not of a new one, and I now produced and read it by short sentences, Mr. Lee interpreting as I went on, and Mr. Phillips and Mr. Betts sitting by to hear the proceedings. The following is a copy:

'Ratification of Grant made verbally by Lo Bengulu, Supreme chief of the Matabili nation, to Mr. Thomas Baines on behalf of the South African Gold Fields Explorations Company Limited on the 9th day of April, 1870.

'I, Lo Bengulu,
    'King of the Matabili nation, do hereby certify that, on the 9th day of April, 1870, in the presence of Mr. John Lee, acting as agent between myself and Mr. Thomas Baines, then and now commanding the Expedition of the South African Gold Fields Exploration Company, Limited, I did freely grant to Mr. Baines, on behalf of the above named Company, full permission to explore, prospect, and dig or mine for gold in all that country lying between the Gwailo river on the South West and the Ganyana river on the North East, and that this my permission includes liberty to build dwelling- and store-houses, to erect machinery for crushing rocks or other necessaries, and for the removal of the gold so obtained; and it also includes all lesser details connected with gold mining.

'In making this grant I did not alienate from my Kingdom this or any other portion of it, but retained intact the Sovereignty of my dominions, and Mr. Baines engaged on behalf of the said Company not to make any claim contrary or injurious to my right as Sovereign of the country, but to recognise my authority as King and to apply to me for such protection as he might require, and I engaged to grant such protection to Mr. Baines as should enable him to enjoy all lawful and proper use of the privileges granted him by me. And I also certify that when, in November of the same year 1870, Mr. Baines asked me what tribute or payment he should make to me in return for said privileges I declined to name any sum, but left it to the judgement of Mr. Baines to make me annually, on behalf of the said Company, such present as might seem proper to him and acceptable to me.

'Among the Matabili the verbal promise of the King has always been regarded as a sufficient guarantee, and many white men now enjoy privileges in virtue of grants made by my father Umseligazi, which I regard as binding on me.

'I also regard my verbal permission given to Mr. Baines as valid

Agreement of mining concession, August 1871
(Extracted from pages 695 and 696 of Thomas Baines's Diary)

and binding on me and my successors, but finding that the customs of white men require that such grants or promises should be made in writing, I now hereby solemnly and fully confirm the grant verbally made to Mr. Baines on behalf of his company.

'In witness of which I hereto append my sign manual,

'Lo Bengula

(Signed) 'His + mark ◯ and seal

'Signed this 29th day of August, 1871.
'Signed same time in witness hereof,

Signed. 'G. A. Phillips.
'F. Betts.
'Robert J. Jewell.
'John Lee.'

As the reading and interpretation proceeded, I could perceive that the king recognised and assented to each paragraph. The long title of our Company rather took his attention, and I believe he had never heard it in full before. Mr. Lee explained it, and told him it was our Company's distinguishing name, just as that to which Mr. Levert belonged was called the London and Limpopo. Also Mr. Lee asked me to repeat the name of the first river, the Gwailo, so that it was quite evident the king thoroughly attended to and understood the document he was about to sign and, in fact, the king complimented me upon my memory in following so closely the very words that he had used, and Mr. Lee also impressed upon him that my recognition of him as king and my protector bound him to afford me his protection, should I require it. The king then signed all the letters and the grant, making the cross in the proper place with his own unaided hand, and he finally impressed the seal that I had made upon each of them, Jewell only spreading the wax for him. He seemed fully to understand that this act marked each letter for his own, and at his request I gave him a supply of wax, with candles and matches, and a bottle of ink for the stamp that I had cut in raised letters. I thanked him for the kind and liberal manner in which he had complied with my request, and told him I hoped to be able to come in next year with the means of working, and I hoped his friendship would continue for many years between us. He said yes, but friendship depended on the conduct of men toward each other for its continuance, and I told him I hoped he would always find my conduct such as it had been hitherto.

Copy of personal letter penned by Henry Hartley on August 20, 1870 on learning of the death of his third-born son, Wille, while elephant hunting near Hartley Hills (Courtesy of Ann-Marie Moore, neé Hartley)

and hope if I live to return that we shall be
more united it has not been my fault, I have done
a little best not much and now the boy I learnt
to love for I miss him in the field as well as camp
and I feel lost give my love to Sarah and may
God bless you is the prayer of your
bereaved
Father
H Carter

Hartley Hill Gold Quartz crushing Company Lim
Port Elizabeth 23d Oct 1874

My Dear Mr Hartley

I have great pleasure in informing you that the Merchants of this town are organising a company under the above title for the purpose of working the reef you shewed me near Hartley Hill Umfuli River. They have already subscribed liberally and I believe mean to carry the work on. They are to buy the machinery of the South African Gold fields company now in Durban and are to take my small battery also — giving me an interest in the company for it. I am not to receive any pay for three years but am to have an interest in the success of the Company. I do not yet know how much but all these matters will be arranged soon. And I intend to devote the greater part of any profit that comes to me perhaps two thirds or three fourths to the payment of such debts as I incurred to such men as yourself, Mr See and others in gaining the concession for the original company.

With regard to that company I am allowed to render it any friendly service that does not injure the interest of the Hartley Hill Co. and if it has discretion enough to avail itself of my friendship I will find it in a way of paying itself yet.

I hope to start from Durban in March and I should be glad to know whether any of your sons or our friends the Jennings are likely to be down and whether they would transport any portion of the machinery either to your farm Thorndale or to Hartley Hill — and at what rates. The distance from Natal to your farm is 475 miles from Durban via Harrismith Sandi's drift in the Vaal River and Potchefstroom — via Heidelburg it is somewhat less. The whole distance from Durban to Hartley Hill via Potchefstroom is 1212 miles

I should like to know specially whether transport can easily be had at reasonable rates from your farm to Hardly Hill – for if this is difficult it will be better for me to buy all my own cattle and wagons in Natal –

I should be glad if you would let me know the price of oxen in the Transvaal in good condition, free from sickness and ready for work –

I expect I shall have to ration from six to nine white men and I shall be glad to take as much of the provision as possible from you – will you let me know the prices of Boers meal pr muid, Salt pork, Bacon, Butter and dried fruit pr 100 lbs – and goats or sheep each.

There will be time to answer this letter – here as I shall certainly stay over November – and perhaps December too, but I shall go to Durban as soon as the business of the Company is settled and I feel that my presence is required there.

I have a picture of "What led to the discovery of the Gold Fields" I sent you a newspaper with a notice of it. Watson recognised your likeness at once and even Mr Robert White formerly of Grahams Town who saw it in Natal recently, asked without any prompting whether that was not Hartley of Bathurst – I will send you a photo. but I think some little of the likeness is lost because the side of the face comes out darker than in the picture.

I am writing to Jewell – he is at Bong Poort Mooi River Natal and has wagons perhaps he may come up with me –

I am quite sure all your friends in Natal would wish me to send their kind regards to you and with my own to all friends and my kindest remembrances to yourself with sincerest sympathy for your late bereavement. Believe me my Dear Mr Hartley

Your very sincere friend and fellow traveller, Baines

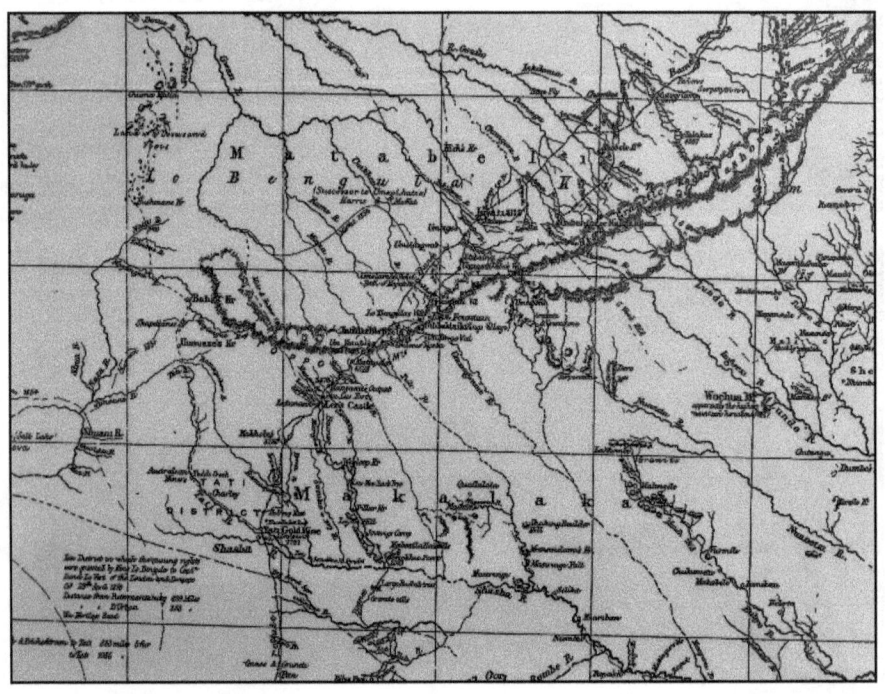

Map of South East African Gold Fields by Thomas Baines of his exploits to 1875

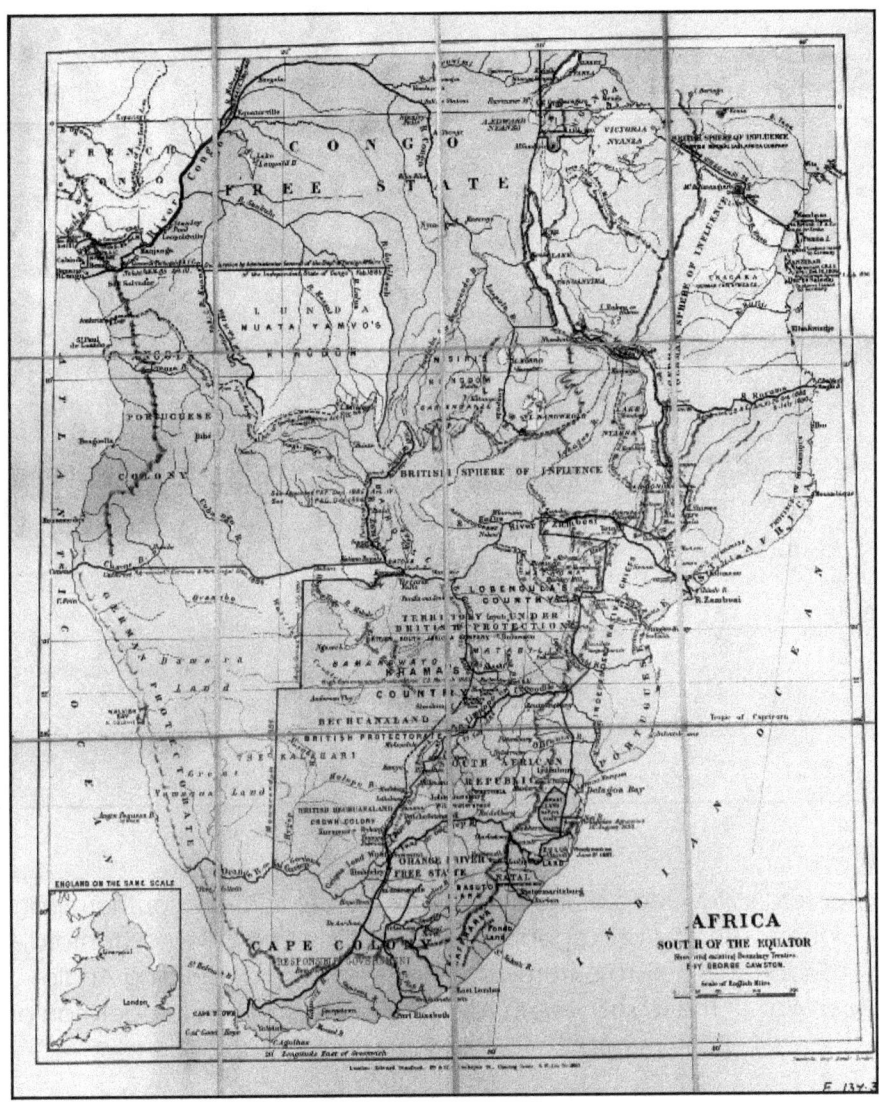

Map of 1884 boundaries of colonial claims. "Africa South of the Equator" published in 1890 (Courtesy of www.RareMaps.com)

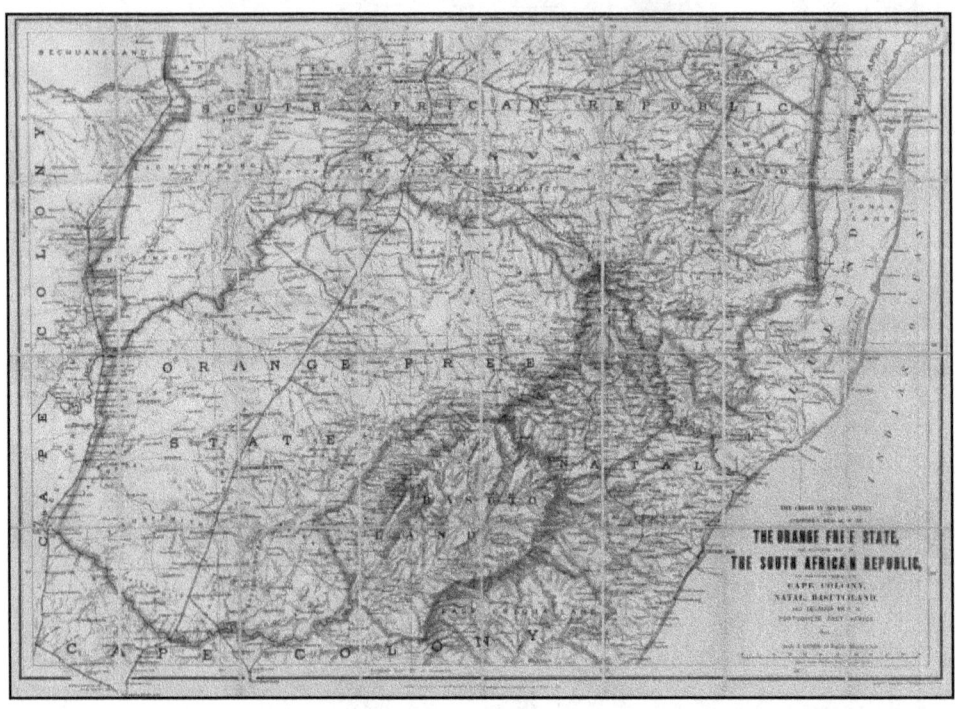

Stanford's New Map of the Orange Free State and the southern part of the South African Republic, 1899, published by Edward Stanford, London, just before outbreak of the Second and deciding Anglo-Boer War – "The Crisis in South Africa" (Courtesy of Barry Ruderman of Barry Lawrence Ruderman Antique Maps Inc.)

Select Bibliography

Acemoglu, Daren and Robinson James A., *Why Nations Fail - the origins of Power, Prosperity and Poverty,* 2012, Penguin Random House, New York

Algar, Frederick, *The Diamond Fields: with notes on the Cape Colony and Natal,* 1872, Historic Print Edition, British Library

Baines, Thomas, F.R.G.S., *The Gold Regions of South Eastern Africa,* 1874, (Facsimile reprint of original)

Baines, Thomas, **Diaries** of 1869-1872, (three volumes) edited by Wallis, J.P.R. 1946, London, Chatto & Windus. (More fully notated as Government Archives of Southern Rhodesia, Oppenheimer Series, *The Northern Goldfields Diaries of Thomas Baines* - First Journey 1869-1870, Volume One; Second Journey 1870-1871, Volume Two; and Second Journey, 1871-1872, Volume Three)

Baines, Thomas, **Journal** of 1877, *The Gold Regions of South Eastern Africa,* Rhodesiana Reprint Library, Volume One - Facsimile reproduction of the 1877 edition - Books of Rhodesia, Bulawayo, 1968

Baines, Thomas, **Papers**. *Original Field Notes of specified dates and Manuscripts.* The Brenthurst Library, Johannesburg

BBC World News, October 22, 2021

Bedford-Hall, Lynn, *Shaka - Warrior King of the Zulus,* 1987 C. Struik Publishers, Cape Town

Bergh, J.S., *S.J.P.Kruger and landownership in the Transvaal* in History 59 (November 2014)

Berrington, Aileen, *The Hartley Story: Thomas Hartley (Senior) and his sons, Thomas Hartley (Junior) & Henry Hartley ('the hunter")* 1987, M&M Printers, Queenstown, eastern Cape Province. (A genealogical family history of descendants)

Bond, John, *They were South Africans,* 1956, Oxford University Press, Cape Town

Bulpin, T.V., *Lost Trails of the Transvaal,* (3rd Edition), 1974, Cape & Transvaal Printers, Cape Town

Bulpin, T.V., *The Ivory Trail,* 1954, Books of Africa (Pty) Ltd., Cape Town

Bulpin, T.V., *To the Banks of the Zambezi,* 1965, Thomas Nelson and Sons (Africa) (Pty) Ltd

Carruthers, Jane & Arnold, Marion, *The Life and Work of Thomas Baines,* 1995, Fernwood Press, South Africa

Carruthers, Jane, *Chapter 11, The Early Boer Republics: Changing Political Forces in the Cradle of Mankind, 1830s to 1890s*, in *A Search for Origins*, 2007, Wits University, Johannesburg

Carruthers, Jane, 'Frederick Jeppe, Mapping of the Transvaal c.1850-1899', (2003) *Journal of Southern African Studies*, published on-line June 3, 2010

De Wet, Conde, & van Heyningen, Elizabeth, (Editors), and van der Merwe, Chris (translator), 2017, *Seleksies uit die Briewe van President M.T. Steyn (1904 -1910)*, Second Series, Van Riebeeck Society, Cape Town

Encyclopedia Britannica, published September 30, 2020

Fitzpatrick, J.P., *The Transvaal from Within. A private record*, 1899, William Heineman, London

Goldswain, Jeremiah, *The Chronicle of Jeremiah Goldswain, 1820 Settler, Memoirs written in 1858*, edited by great grandson Ralph Goldswain in 2014 – self published

Hartley Family Bible, 1846, (courtesy of Simon Hartley in Rustenburg, Magaliesberg, South Africa)

Hockly, H.E., *The Story of British Settlers of 1820 to South Africa*, (Second Edition) 1957, Juta & Co., Cape Town

Holmes, Prescott, *Paul Kruger. The Life Story of the President of the Transvaal*, 1900, Henry Altemus, Philadelphia

Kanfer, Stefan, *The Last Empire – De Beers, Diamonds and the World*, 1993, Harper Collins, Canada.

Kieser, A., *President Steyn in die Krisisjare 1896–1899*, (1939) Bloemfontein, Nasionale Boekhandel Bpk., Kaapstad

Le Roux, Servaas, D., *Pioneers and Sportsmen of South Africa*, 1939, Salisbury, Southern Rhodesia

Leask, Thomas, *Southern African Diaries of 1865–1870*, edited by Wallis, J.P.R., 1954, Chatto & Windus, London

Map of The Gold Fields of South Eastern Africa, 1876, by T. Baines, F.RG.S, assisted by James Chapman, Henry Hartley, et al, published by Edward Stanford, London

Map: *First Edition of Regional Map of South Africa & neighbouring regions*, published by Stanford Maps during *"The Crisis in South Africa in 1899"*. London

Mohr, Eduard, *To the Victoria Falls of the Zambezi*, 1876, translated from the German, facsimile reproduction

Pakenham, Thomas, *The Scramble for Africa*, 1991, Johnathan Ball Publishers, Johannesburg

Pictoral History of South Africa, 1938, published by Odhams Press Ltd. Longacre, London. No author

Reitz, Deneys, *Trilogy, Adrift on the Open Veld – The Anglo-Boer War and its aftermath 1899–1943* (Reprinted as *The Deneys Reitz Trilogy*, 2011), Plumstead, Cape Town

Rhodesiana, collection of memorabilia on the Internet, (no date)

Ritter, E.A., *Shaka Zulu*, 1955, Longmans, Cape Town

Rosenthal, Eric, *Encyclopedia of Southern Africa* (Seventh edition) 1978, Juta & Co. Cape Town

Sanders, Muriel H., *Glimpses of the Past*, 1973, on Jennings family history from nearby Nooitgedacht farm in the Magaliesberg Valley

Thackeray, Reginald (Captain) "Hartley" Thackeray, *Henry Hartley: African Hunter and Explorer,* appearing in the Journal of the Royal African Society of July 1938, Oxford University Press

Tucker, Michael, *Zimbabwe History Society* and author of the www.Zimfieldguide.com website

Van Zÿl, Jan, *Bethule 1896-1907, met spesifieke verwysing na die Anglo Boeroolog.* Doctoral Thesis, Universiteit van die Vrystaat, November, 2019, Bloemfontein

Walker, Eric, A., (General Editor) *Cambridge History of the British Empire, Volume VIII, South Africa* (Second Edition), 1963, Cambridge University Press

Walker, Eric, A., *Historic Atlas of South Africa,* 1922, Oxford University Press, Humphrey Milford, Cape Town

Wheatcraft, Geoffrey, *The Randlords – the exploits and explorations of South African Mining Magnets,* 1984, published by author

York, Geoffrey, & Moya, Jeffery, *The Globe & Mail newspaper* of January 12, 2022

York, Geoffrey, *The Globe & Mail newspaper* of May 29, 2021

Index (select)

Anglo-Boer War - 11, 16, 21, 38, 43, 60, 72, 86, 89, 108-11, 116, 126
Baines, Thomas - 11, 15-6, 21, 29, 32, 42, 46-7, 50, 54, 57-59, 61, 63, 65-8, 71, 73-5, 77-9, 81-107, 110, 113-4, 120, 122, 124, 133
Barotseland - 40, 89
Bathurst, E. Cape - 10, 15, 19, 26-7, 29, 32, 35-6, 40, 55, 81, 89
Bechuanaland (Botswana) - 10, 20, 46, 49, 50, 57, 63, 81, 85, 89, 96, 101, 103, 114, 121, 127-8, 130, 133
Berrington, Aileen - 26, 60, 61-5, 119
Botha, Louis - 110, 116
Bulawayo - 10-1, 21, 32, 41-2, 45, 50, 56-7, 75-6, 86, 98, 102-5, 111, 124
Calton, Dr - 23-4, 26, 55
Chaplin, Arthur J - 61
Chapman, James - 58-9
Coverley, Dr - 64, 81
Crejan - 64-5
East London - 27, 41, 73
Frontier wars - 10, 19, 32, 35-6, 74
Goldswain, Jeremiah - 35, 37
Grahamstown (Makhanda) - 20, 25, 27-8, 30, 35, 40-2, 44-5, 60, 73, 81, 89, 121
Great Fish River - 24-7, 32, 35-8
Great Kei River - 36-7
Groot Marico - 45, 49
Harare (Salisbury) - 41, 56-7, 76, 83
Hartley (not Henry)
  Frederick - 21, 29-30, 32, 49, 52, 56, 60, 64, 89, 102, 106, 108-9, 112-4, 117

Henry Albert Rorke (Harry, son) - 21, 30, 101-2, 108-9, 114-7, 119
Mary Elizabeth (daughter) - 29
Reginald Henry - 41
Sarah Ann (daughter) - 29
Sarah Green (mother) - 23
Simon - 50, 55, 85, 117, 119
Thomas (father) - 10, 23, 25-6, 33, 35
Thomas, jnr (brother) - 28, 35, 55, 61
Thomas John (son) - 11, 21, 29-30, 52, 60, 64, 108-10, 116-7
Willie/William (son) - 11, 21, 29-30, 32, 52, 60, 64-5, 93, 97, 99, 108, 112-3, 115, 117
Hartley Hills - 11, 21, 29, 39, 41, 56, 61, 64-5, 71, 77, 79, 81, 83-5, 88, 92, 96-8, 104-5, 107, 112, 115, 119
Jameson, Dr - 75
Jewell, RJ - 66, 81, 87, 99, 104, 106-7, 113
Kimberley - 11, 86-7, 92, 102
Kidson, Emma Witcomb - 10, 28-9
Kruger, Paul - 20, 44-5, 48, 50-1, 61, 112, 117, 121, 123
Leask, Thomas - 16-7, 33, 42, 59, 61, 63, 65, 97, 113, 115
Lee, John - 59, 63, 80
Lee (missionary) - 93, 102
Livingstone, David - 10, 15, 47, 56-9, 123
Lobengula - 11, 13, 15, 20, 32, 43, 50, 56, 74-5, 77-8, 82, 86, 92-93, 95-6, 102, 104 107-8, 114, 123

Magaliesberg - 10-1, 21, 29, 39, 44-5, 49, 50, 53, 55, 57, 60, 64, 72, 77, 104-5, 107-9, 111, 113, 117, 119, 127

Maloney, Emily Sarah (stepdaughter) - 108, 113

Maloney, Mary Ann (wife) - 10, 30, 49, 81, 101

Maloney, Tom (adopted son) - 30, 49, 60, 64, 97, 99, 106, 108, 116

Mandela, Nelson - 38, 73, 128

Mansfield, England - 10, 23

Maqoma (chief) - 35

Mashonaland - 11, 19-20, 40, 43, 74-5, 77, 79, 86, 89, 92, 107, 124

Matabeleland - 10-1, 15, 19-21, 30, 32, 40, 42, 46, 49-50, 60-1, 74-5, 77, 79, 84, 86-7, 89, 92, 102, 106-9, 115, 120-1, 124

Mauch, Karl - 11, 20, 42, 50, 59, 71-2, 79, 84

Mbeki, Thabo - 38-9

Mnangagwa, Emmerson - 76, 94, 125

Mohr, Eduard - 17, 42, 54, 58, 61, 63, 65, 70, 79, 81, 90, 106

Mugabe, Robert - 38, 76, 94, 98

Mzilikazi - 10-1, 15, 20, 32, 42, 45-6, 50, 54, 56-8, 61, 74, 77-8, 84-5, 92-3, 95, 108, 120-1, 123

Natal/Zululand (incl Pietermaritzburg) - 11, 21, 37, 39, 40-1, 45-6, 58, 61, 72, 75, 77, 79-81, 86-9, 96, 100-1, 106-7, 110, 115-6, 121, 123, 129

Nelson, CJ - 87

Nkomo, Joshua - 76, 98, 125

Nongqawuse - 36-7

Oliver, Mr - 104-5, 107

Port Elizabeth (Gqeberha) - 19, 27, 40-1, 50, 52, 55, 73, 80, 89, 92, 130

Potchefstroom - 20, 28, 40-1, 44-5, 57, 60, 70, 73, 87, 88-9

Pretorius, Andries - 41, 75

Queen Victoria - 20, 29, 44, 50, 58, 75, 124

Ramaphosa, Cyril - 39, 118, 129

Rustenburg - 20, 41, 44-5, 48, 55, 60, 89-90, 101, 103-4, 109, 111, 117-8

Rhodes, Cecil John - 20, 42, 75, 82, 92, 102, 107, 124-5

Sechele (chief) - 47

Shaka Zulu - 20, 45-6, 92, 123, 129

Shepstone, Theophiles - 7

Smith, Ian - 76, 94, 98, 127

Swinburne, John - 42, 84-5, 87

Thackeray, Joseph William - 41

Thackeray, Reginald Hartley - 41, 56, 59, 64

Thorndale - 10-1, 16, 20-1, 29-30, 39, 41, 44, 49, 50-2, 57, 60, 64-5, 72-3, 79-81, 84, 86-7, 100, 102-11, 116, 117, 119, 129

Transvaal (not Magaliesberg) - 10, 20-1, 30, 32, 40-2, 44-51, 57, 60-1, 72, 74, 77, 79-80, 89, 103, 104, 106-11, 115, 120, 121, 126

Upton, Elizabeth Hope - 10, 30

Van der Byl, PK - 59

Verseput, Cécile - 51

Verwoerd, Hendrik - 111-2, 127

Victoria Falls - 10, 56-9, 70, 78, 86, 90, 106

Zuma, Jacob - 39, 129

www.ingramcontent.com/pod-product-compliance
Lightning Source LLC
Chambersburg PA
CBHW071438160426
43195CB00013B/1946